BRIG

THE DIARY OF A YOUNG GIRL BY ANNE FRANK

Intelligent Education

INFLUENCE PUBLISHERS

Nashville, Tennessee

BRIGHT NOTES: The Diary of a Young Girl

www.BrightNotes.com

No part of this publication may be used or reproduced in any manner whatsoever without written permission, except in the case of brief quotations in critical articles and reviews. For permissions, contact Influence Publishers http://www.influencepublishers.com.

ISBN: 978-1-645420-24-8 (Paperback)
ISBN: 978-1-645420-25-5 (eBook)

Published in accordance with the U.S. Copyright Office Orphan Works and Mass Digitization report of the register of copyrights, June 2015.

Originally published by Monarch Press.
Eugenie Harris, 1965
2019 Edition published by Influence Publishers.

Interior design by Lapiz Digital Services. Cover Design by Thinkpen Designs.

Printed in the United States of America.

Library of Congress Cataloging-in-Publication Data forthcoming.
Names: Intelligent Education
Title: BRIGHT NOTES: The Diary of a Young Girl
Subject: STU004000 STUDY AIDS / Book Notes

CONTENTS

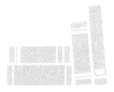

INTRODUCTION TO ANNE FRANK

. . . .

EARLIEST LIFE

More difficult than condensing an author's biography is the prospect of enlarging upon the tragically short one of Anne Frank. Born in Frankfort am Main, Germany, on June 12, 1929, Annelies Marie Frank was the second daughter of a well-to-do middle-class Jewish family. Her sister Margot was three years her senior. Otto Frank, Anne's father, was eleven years older than his wife, and both parents had come from very wealthy backgrounds. The Frank family lived in Germany resisting the growing pressures of Adolf Hitler's campaign to wipe out the Jews until 1933, when it was no longer tolerable nor safe to remain there.

EMIGRATION TO HOLLAND

When Anne was four years old, her family moved to Amsterdam where they lived quite pleasantly among the sympathetic Dutch, Christians, and Jews alike, for the next several years. In business, Mr. Frank prospered as Managing Director of the firm Travies N.V., serving also as a partner in the firm of Kolen and Company. The Franks made many friends, some of whom were later to risk their lives to protect the family when Hitler eventually spread his ugly program for the Jews into Holland.

Anne attended the Montessori School in Amsterdam for the next six years. Then it was made apparent to her and the other Jewish children that somehow they were different and would thenceforth have to attend special schools. The transfer of Anne to the Jewish Lyceum in 1940 marks the beginning of a period of increasing travail for the Franks and others against whom Hitler's anti-Jewish laws were directed. For in May of that year the Nazis invaded the Netherlands, and in a matter of days, all Dutch resistance was crushed save for extremely risky underground activities.

NAZI OCCUPATION

The discriminatory regulations of the Nazis restricted virtually every privilege of the Jews, from transportation and education, to entertainment and commerce. In fact, all Jews were designated as a separate people by a special law requiring them to wear a yellow six-pointed Star of David which was to be prominently displayed at all times. The Franks were well aware of the temper of the times. Although they continued for two more years to live what seemed a normal life on the surface, plans for a change were carefully being calculated by Mr. Frank and a close group of friends. Each day strands of an invisible web were being woven about the group in preparation for their eventual "disappearance." The choice would soon have to be made-whether to yield to arrest and ultimate removal to concentration camps, or to take matters into their own hands and hide, as flight from Nazi-infested Europe was no longer possible. With the Gestapo (Hitler's police force) stalking the streets of Amsterdam in search of Jewish prey whom they "summoned" on the flimsiest pretext, July, 1942, brought sad but swift fulfillment to the Frank's plans.

IN HIDING

With moments to spare, the family embarked upon their last free walk along the streets of Amsterdam. In a seemingly ordinary manner so as not to rouse suspicion, they greeted people they knew along the way. Carrying ordinary looking satchels filled with immediate personal belongings, they journeyed in a pouring summer rain the short distance to their hiding place. On July 9, 1942, they ventured to a building located on the Prinsengracht, one of the city's canals. At the rear of the third floor was a disguised apartment in which the Franks and another family named Van Daan remained in self-imposed exile for the next two years. It is during this period that Anne wrote her diary which reveals not only an extraordinary literary talent for one so young, but which has provided the world with a valuable firsthand document of World War II.

DISCOVERED

On August 4, 1944, the Gestapo raided the apartment hideout. They searched the quarters demanding for confiscation anything which they considered to be of value. The Diary was spilled out of Otto Frank's briefcase along with other papers the Gestapo considered unimportant. It lay on the floor among a pile of books and papers until it was found later by friends who preserved it. All of the occupants of the apartment were arrested and sent to German concentration camps. Of the two families, only Otto Frank survived. Two friends who had served as links to the outside were also arrested and sent to Dutch concentration camps. Enduring their imprisonment, they were able to return to their families. Anne herself died at Bergen-Belsen, a German concentration camp, in March, 1945, just two months before both her sixteenth birthday and the Allied liberation of Holland.

HOW AND WHY IT HAPPENED

If there is any explanation possible for the atrocities against humanity committed during World War II by the Hitler Regime (the Third Reich), it lies in historical facts which combined freakishly to produce such acts on the parts of many people. An understanding is required of social and economic conditions which constitute the underlying causes of war before the immediate causes can begin to be understood. And, once war has begun, the actions of all involved people often lie beyond moral or rational considerations. There is no suitable answer to "why" in cases like that of Anne Frank and her family. Man's inhumanity to man can never be explained away. Nevertheless, a brief look at the conditions which gave rise to a "Fuehrer" (leader) like the fanatical Adolf Hitler will help the approach to an interpretation of that historical phenomenon.

HISTORICAL BACKGROUND

Economics

Although all European countries were hard hit after 1929 by a general economic depression, the plight of Germany was by far the worst. The Versailles Treaty of 1919, which ended World War I, had left Germany economically crippled as punishment for being guilty of the war according to the victor nations. Stripped of her colonial possessions and internationally humiliated, she was made responsible for the war debt by means of enormous and somewhat unrealistic reparations payments to the Allies (Serbia, France, Belgium, England, The United States, Japan, and Montenegro). While countries such as England and the United States sought a compromise in the making of payments so that Germany could restore a degree of economic health, France and Belgium punished their neighbor for defaulting in payments by occupying the industrial section of Germany known as the Ruhr. World economic conditions were such that strikes occurred among workers of all nations. When German workers acted similarly, production of goods ceased, and Germany declared bankruptcy. To alleviate the situation, an international committee was set up to consider the problem. The result was the adoption of the Dawes Plan which enabled Germany to borrow money from other countries and thus to stabilize finances. When she did again begin to make reparations payments, France and Belgium withdrew their troops from the Ruhr. There was still considerable pressure on Germany to keep up in her payments to the other Allies who owed money to the United States for loans made to finance World War I. Thus, Germany seemed to be in an interminable economic bind.

Politics

The trend in Europe after World War I was one of liberalism and democratic government. In 1918 the imperial system ended in Germany when local princes abdicated. In 1919 the formation of the Weimar Republic was accomplished by the ratification of a democratic constitution. This did not guarantee peace from within, as factions on the Left and Right still struggled for power in the weaknesses of the infant Republic. There was considerable dissatisfaction over the humiliations suffered by Germany in accepting the terms of the Treaty of Versailles.

Revolts and other attempts to overthrow the government were common. By 1928 much of this inner turmoil had been settled, and Germany was beginning to see daylight with Paul von Hindenburg, initially a capable man, as President. After the onset of the 1929 depression, once again extremist groups rattled the political stability of the barely recuperating Republic of Germany.

Hitler's Rise

Similar to cases of other newly democratized European countries, Germany's story of how a dictatorship was born is a typical example. Economic threats caused panic among rapidly splintering groups of citizens whose only thought in common was to find security and stability. Such social and economic conditions brought about a loss of faith in the Weimar Republic and the capability of its aging President Hindenburg. Renewed bitterness against the Versailles Treaty which he continued to support paved the way for the spread of a fanatical new nationalism. Embodying this spirit was Adolf Hitler, a maladjusted World War I veteran who harbored a maniacal hatred for democracy, trade unions, Jews and Communists in particular. He had an almost equal dislike for Socialists and Catholics, as well as any other elements or individuals not of purely German (Aryan) origin. His party, the Germany National-Social Workers' (NAZI), had attempted once before in 1923 to seize power from the shaky young Weimar Republic, but the plot had failed and he had been imprisoned. In 1929, however, conditions were ripe for such a man as Hitler, whose almost hypnotic powers of persuasion could sway a frightened and disillusioned people. The Nazi Party's growth was spectacular, and by 1933 Hitler had gained enough popular support for a reluctant Hindenburg to entrust him with the post of Chancellor.

From this point on the usurpation of control was relatively easy, and Hitler lost no time in establishing his dictatorship.

Hitler's Program

Hitler's avowed purpose was to re-establish Germany's place of power and prestige among the nations of the world and to restore economic stability by reviving industry and agriculture. His terms for achieving this were based on three main objectives: 1) the negation of the Versailles Treaty; 2) The creation of a strong economic and military Germany; and 3) the elimination of Communist, Jewish, and all other "non-German" interests. This program appealed widely to a basically proud people brought to its knees by international degradation and economic chaos. German youth was especially receptive to Hitler's plans and worked enthusiastically toward his goals, for they had known little if anything of German glory in their lifetimes. If members of the older generation were reluctant to embrace the fanatical surge of this new nationalism, they maintained an attitude of indifference or passive acceptance for a while, feeling that social and economic conditions warranted improvement by almost any workable means. Soon it became apparent that the only attitude possible under the Hitler regime was acceptance and willing participation whether out of enthusiasm or fear. For in June, 1934, the people were taught an object lesson in the execution of some few hundred suspected by the Fuehrer of opposition to his program.

Hitler's Information Service

Hitler's public relations policy was to seem to his people to be everywhere at once. Enlarged photographs of the Fuehrer were almost inescapable as were "swastikas" (the Nazi emblem). Hitler's propaganda machine, administered by Dr. Joseph Goebbels, was a most important tool for keeping the people informed. Having seized control of mass communications early in his dictatorship, he had the twofold power of being able to suppress whatever information might threaten the Reich's policies and to spread those ideas which would benefit them. In these ways, he forced adherence to his program by controlling the thinking of an entire nation. As time went on, the methods and activities of the Nazis developed unbelievably inhuman aspects. Nevertheless, such distorted information was disseminated concerning these horrors that an entire populace was only vaguely aware of what was actually happening. The outside world was mystified. Except for rumors, only Hitler and his closest henchmen who were sworn to secrecy knew the lurid certainties of what was in store for those out of favor with the Reich.

Prejudice And Persecution

Hitler was a powerful orator whose extraordinary ability to rouse people to frenzied action remains an undisputed fact. He was shrewd enough to disguise those aspects of his personality which have since been recognized as sick by exploiting nationalistic sentiment. He was clever enough to make his own distorted desires appear to be the goals of Germany. His ability to twist historical facts enabled him to convince the masses that Jews, Communists, Socialists, and Catholics were responsible for Germany's misfortunes. Jews, he maintained, had encouraged acceptance of the Versailles Treaty in order to protect their economic interests abroad and were greedy enough to be able to wring profit from the war debt. He emphasized the fact that Jews were not truly of German blood, and could never be considered loyal Germans with a history of wandering behind them. The Communists were Hitler's political opponents, and he stressed their affiliations with the Soviets, thus making them into agents of foreign interests. Socialists, too, as part of an international movement were discredited and vilified. The Catholics' religious loyalty to Rome was the unfavorable issue he exploited where that group was concerned. Hitler's aim was to "purify" the German population of these and all non-Aryan elements. By attributing the ills of the nation to them he efficiently created these groups into the collective national scapegoat. With the temper of the people sufficiently inflamed, he could do pretty much as he chose with the scapegoat and count on adequate support. What deeper prejudices lay behind his policies is a matter about which there has been much speculation.

Foreign Policy And War

What information leaked out of Germany concerning internal affairs horrified the world, but no one was terribly eager to antagonize this powerful and frightening dictator so long as he kept his activities confined within the boundaries of his own country. Appalled by bits and pieces of news about the fate of a few unfortunate individuals, the Allies were more concerned by the disturbing advent of totalitarian governments in Italy, Russia, and Japan. These dictatorships, along with Germany, threatened to upset the status quo in international affairs. It was still hoped that the League of Nations could preserve the peace and the balance of power in Europe. The Geneva Disarmament Conference of 1932–1934 was intended to correct the failure to disarm of those nations who had promised to do so in the Versailles Treaty. So alarmed at Hitler's rise to power and the menace presented by the potential military strength of the Third Reich, these nations could not come to any terms of agreement on arms reduction at the sacrifice of their safety. In 1933, Hitler blasted all hopes for an easing of European tensions by withdrawing from both the Geneva Conference and the League of Nations. The withdrawals were his means of retaliation for a refusal of his request for a revision of the Versailles Treaty. In 1935 he boldly announced Germany's intention to rearm. Still nervous about the Reich's lack of a strong European ally, he held his aggressive aspirations in check until an agreement known as the "Axis" was established with Italy in 1936.

Nazi infiltration into countries where German minorities existed had been quietly in progress since 1933. Hitler's aim was to unite all German peoples into a "Greater Germany," comprised of the German-populated areas of other European countries, and ultimately to wield total authority himself from Berlin. In March, 1938, Austria became a German province. In September of that year he annexed the Sudeten portion of Czechoslovakia, proclaiming in April, 1939, another portion of that country as a German "protectorate." Having agreed to divide Poland with Russia in a non-aggression pact, in September, 1939, Germany invaded that nation, whom France and Britain had agreed to protect. The result of the invasion of Poland was the declaration of war on Germany by the French and British. In April, 1940, Hitler's troops accomplished the occupation of Denmark and Norway in a single day. In May, the Germans invaded Belgium and the Netherlands. The Dutch resistance lasted four days, whereupon Queen Wilhelmina and the government fled to seek asylum in England. The Belgians held out for eighteen days under King Leopold. By June, Hitler had subdued France and had established the Occupational (Vichy) Government of Marshal Petain. Although not so-called until December, 1941, these battles constituted the early stages of World War II.

Pinpointing The Jews

As early as 1933, the Jews in Germany were victimized by discriminatory legislation by which their position degenerated over the next six years from secondary citizenship to non-citizenship, and finally, to virtual non-existence. The "Jewish Question," as Hitler referred to it, was an issue carried over from the early days of the Nazi Party's program of 1920. More than simply an aspect of early Nazism, to Hitler, a solution to the "Jewish Question" was a goal of paramount importance. As anti-Jewish legislation became an increasing reality in Germany from 1933 to 1938, many Jews left the country early in the decade with relative freedom. More Jews, however, remained there in a fool's paradise, thinking that the presently lenient emigration policy would permit them to leave if and when they chose to do. On the basis of family ties, wealth, possessions, and careers, there was less of a desire to emigrate than there was to endure current discrimination. Many Jews even looked upon Germany as their homeland, and felt, as "true" Germans, that the revolutionary measures of the Nazis were only temporary.

The First Solution

In 1938 the "First Solution" to the "Jewish Question" was enacted with startling swiftness. In a word, it was expulsion. The wealthier Jews had little difficulty in leaving; the poorer ones could not so easily afford the costs of proper documents or transportation. With a fortnight allotted them to emigrate, these less affluent people looked for guidance to Jewish "functionaries" who were working with the Nazis on the problem of relocation. The black-marketing of passports was on the rise, as were bribery, forgery, theft, and other measures of desperation necessarily taken by those with a price on their heads. Some

Jews attempted to renounce their religion, either by conversion or by falsified birth certificates. Others were willing to remain in Germany whatever the penalty if just one family member's salvation could be acquired. Escape by underground methods became more and more frequent.

In the early days of emigration, Jews had found an area of relocation to be more or less a matter of choice. The selection of neighboring nations such as Holland, Belgium, France, and England was both logical and commonly practiced. Some scattered even to Scandinavia or British-held Palestine. There were those who ventured as far as Canada, South America, and the United States. Some difficulties were connected with the immigration laws of their adopted countries, but for the most part, the early emigres were rather easily resettled. After the 1938 decree, the wealthier Jews found relocation more difficult, but the poorer Jews were faced not only with lack of funds for transportation, but they had virtually no place to go. The officials of the Jewish communities, Jews themselves, attempted to select a destination arbitrarily which, as often as not, was felt by those upon whom the edict had been thrust to be as unpalatable as remaining in Germany. Torn between the alternatives offered by their own leaders and the Nazis, these individuals were helpless and stranded.

The Second Solution

With still too many Jews remaining in Germany to suit him, Hitler enacted what he termed the "Second Solution." Between 1938 and 1939 those who could procure no papers or find no place of relocation or were still in Germany for some other reason were sent to concentration camps until their fate could be decided.

Many Jews took to hiding, sometimes aided by sympathetic friends and neighbors. The Jewish "functionaries" who felt exempt from danger by virtue of their work for the Reich, and who for a while longer believed that they were helping their people to avoid committing crimes against the administration, sought out fellow Jews in hiding and rounded them up for the concentration camps. Sympathizers when discovered were punished as political criminals and likewise deported to the camps.

The Camps

Little was known about the concentration camps at first, except that for the expelled Jews remaining in Germany, they were areas of temporary location until Hitler could decide what to do with them. It was thought that perhaps German penal colonies in remote regions of the globe would be established as a possible answer to the problem of relocation. Meanwhile, those interned in the camps were occupied with forced labor and other less attractive activities which ranged from serving as specimens for experimental medicine to being made a sport for their keepers' whims of brutality and perversion. Prisoners of all ages were herded across the landscape to the camps in cattle cars. Upon arrival, they were segregated according to the function in which they could best serve the Reich. Family ties meant nothing, nor did other human considerations. Of course, the weakest died first. Conditions for survival were at a minimum. Germany could not afford food and other materials required for use during a time of impending war on such as Jews. Often, those prisoners suffering from malnutrition, disease, or other symptoms of physical decline were the victims of "mercy killings."

The Final Solution

By 1939 Hitler's aggressive tactics in international affairs had plunged Germany into the initial phases of World War II. Wartime economy as well as war psychology demanded a "Final Solution" to the "Jewish Question." This, in a word, meant extermination. All Jews in Germany and German-occupied countries were to be annihilated. "Experts" on the "Jewish Question" such as Adolf Eichmann and others were consulted. Removal of the Jews to remote places was now a discarded plan because of the impossibilities of wartime transportation. There was just one answer, and under Hitler's orders, all Jews were to be rounded up and sent to certain camps where special equipment was being built for their extermination.

Shooting took too long and would utilize ammunition needed for the war. Starvation was too slow. Inflicting disease was too dangerous to those unscheduled for death. Poisoning was not an unsuitable idea, but how could it be most efficiently accomplished among six million Jews? It was then decided that enormous gas chambers be constructed to resemble ordinary buildings large enough to contain hundreds, and in some cases, thousands of people. These buildings would contain outlets for the poison gas which would be piped in and controlled from the outside by valves. In a few hours when asphyxiation was complete, the corpses could be removed and a new batch of prisoners who had been promised "showers" before relocating could be locked in for the next gassing. The disposals of the corpses at first presented another problem. It was soon solved. As burying thousands of bodies was impractical, cremating the remains was decided upon. Huge crematoriums were erected near the gas chambers. These decisions made, the "Final Solution" went into effect in 1941.

Occupied Holland And The Jews

The Jewish population of the Netherlands in 1942 was approximately one hundred and forty thousand. Of these, some thirty-five thousand were "stateless" Jews, a term meaning that they were refugees, mostly from Germany. The Dutch had been openly hostile to the anti-Jewish measures taken by the Nazis since the occupation of Holland in 1940. When, in 1942, the programming of the "Final Solution" went into effect in the Netherlands, it meant the initial deportation of twenty thousand Jews to concentration camps. To this enactment, there was violent opposition among the Dutch in the form of a wave of strikes.

The sympathy of the Dutch for the Jews was threatened in two ways. First, that segment of the population involved in the Nazi movement formed a very powerful machine. Ever loyal to the Fuehrer and his Aryan ideals, the Dutch Nazis could be counted upon to unearth Jews from their hiding places, whence seizure and deportation were immediately carried out. Secondly, among the Jews themselves, there existed a cleavage between the native-born and the refugees. The native Jews were led to believe that it was only the foreigners who were to be the victims of Hitler's plans. To save themselves, many Dutch-born Jews were easily enlisted by the Nazis into a Jewish police force, an agency of a larger body known as the Jewish Council. Similar to Caesar's method of "divide and conquer," this pitting of Jew against Jew succeeded in the eventual deportation by July, 1944, of one hundred and thirteen thousand Jews. This figure included a larger percentage of native Dutch Jews whose collaboration with the Nazis proved a catastrophe out of proportion to anything these duped people could possibly have imagined. For, even among the twenty thousand Jews who survived in hiding, only five thousand were Dutch born.

THE DIARY OF A YOUNG GIRL

. . . .

SIGNIFICANCE OF ANNE FRANK'S DIARY

William Wordsworth wrote in his "Ode on the Intimations of Immortality," (1803–06), of the unusual perception of children. An excerpt from stanza VII contains the lines, "Mighty Prophet! Seer blest!/ On whom those truths do rest / which we are toiling all our lives to find /." And well these phrases pertain to Anne Frank, an unknown youngster, confiding her most private thoughts to her diary, a make-believe friend she had named "Kitty." Groping her way through the confused years of early adolescence, Anne was not only brave enough to ask "why?" regarding the ways of human nature, but perceptive enough to begin ferreting out some of the most important answers to questions man asks himself about his fellow creatures.

Ironically aided by the gruesome conditions of war, Anne was provided with a firsthand observation of mankind engaged in acts of the rawest reality. She was able to formulate from among these observations certain conclusions regarding the nature of man generally, as well as man specifically under conditions of duress. What is so remarkable about this young girl's perception, was her ability to handle some of the most complicated answers to life's questions-questions which even many adults do not wish to ask. In addition to her unusually keen ability to understand, was her heroic strength in being able to both find and accept the truth. For, despite the tendency of the young to distort their viewpoint so that the self is exclusively in focus, Anne's vision was broad enough to include not only a growing awareness of herself, but to incorporate, in amazingly accurate perspective, herself in a field of relationships, broadening from those of immediate family and companions to humanity as a whole. Aside from her capabilities of awareness, was her exceptional ability to judge herself and others, if not always favorably, at least with an untutored wisdom that would be envied by the highest tribunals.

What evolves from the pages of Anne's diary is a philosophy of life that is rare, not only for such a young person, but especially unusual for any individual subjected to the ugliness of war. Such threats to existence and degradation of the human spirit do not ordinarily produce the positive attitude with which Anne faced her circumstances. What this reveals is the true nobility of the soul. It is the will not only to go on in a semiexistence diseased by fear and hatred, but the will to go on making every moment count, and above all, the will to survive beyond the moment. Despite the horrors and humiliations of each day, the constantly alternating factors of salvation and disaster, and the unbalanced elements of good and evil, Anne's was a spiritual force of unusual drive and direction. The existence of such spiritual strength occurs only in individuals of vastly rich inner resources.

Some few people among the earth's millions are born so generously supplied with these inner riches; others, perhaps, are able to cultivate them. Of either group, there are more who do not utilize them than those who do. Why this is so is less important than the immense value to the world of those richly endowed people who share their gifts and talents with their fellow man. Of this group, it is more commonly those who, having reached adulthood, can most effectively benefit others. The uncommon cases are the exceptionally talented or "precocious" children, and thus, more valued their gifts. Some precocious children are exploited by their elders, or otherwise spoiled by their own consciousness of early fame. This was never so with Anne Frank, who, unknown to anyone, confided naively in a diary. She died before the age of sixteen, unaware that her diary would become not only a famous work of non-fiction literature, but a seriously studied document of World War II, and in addition, a Broadway play and a Hollywood film.

CHILDREN AND LITERATURE

From our earliest years, we are accustomed to the appearance of children in literature. At first, they speak through the metaphor of their experiences in fairy tales and nursery rhymes. This progresses to youthful stories in which young people, then our contemporaries, enact the adventures we ourselves may not have, but with which we may identify. Such books are designed to encourage the projection of ourselves into the roles of imaginary counterparts whose escapades amuse us. Another function these books serve is to teach us, through our imaginary counterparts, some lessons of life, particularly concepts behavior and values, which seem for the youthful heroes and heroines in the pages of books more pleasantly learned than by direct parental counseling. There are dozens of books of this sort, written by adults for children, which have assumed the stature of classical literature for young readers. The names of Louisa May Alcott, Robert Louis Stevenson, Mark Twain, Charles Dickens, the Brothers Grimm, and Hans Christian Andersen are just a few among the many authors whose works are considered standard reading for children.

As we mature we may find that those same children who appeared to be ourselves in the reading of our youth now serve another function. As our values progress toward adulthood, those children are no longer objects of identification but ones of reflection for our maturing concept of the world. We are better able to discriminate between the values of youth and adulthood, and the children in such works as Twain and Dickens, for instance, assume for us a greatly altered position in terms of their values. We learn, much to our surprise, that Lewis Carroll's *Alice in Wonderland*, far from being the simple narrative of a young girl's sleeping fantasy, is a complicated work of satire, and Alice, herself, an instrument of the author's social criticism. The same may be said for Barrie's Peter Pan, but not in the satirical sense, so much as in the notion of its importance as an idealized philosophy of childhood.

Not only does the literature of childhood acquire a new dimension in retrospect as the reader's maturity develops, but books for more adult readers employ children as characters by which other attitudes may be examined. For instance, George Eliot's *Silas Marner* employs the child Eppie as the most important factor in the old weaver's reacceptance of society from which he had voluntarily exiled himself. Harper Lee's *To Kill A Mockingbird* examines some aspects of racial prejudice in terms of the children, Jem and Scout. Authors reflect upon their childhood experiences in novels and short stories in which autobiography is transformed into fiction. Such authors, as James Joyce, Thomas Mann, D. H. Lawrence, and Thomas Wolfe reflect attitudes and experiences they had in growing up by means of children, not unlike their own young selves, whom they have created to serve their art.

What makes the children in these works of such importance as characters is their extraordinary sensitivity and perception. In other words, they are the precocious children whose prophetic wisdom and insight into life endows them with a vision of humanity from which adults might learn. Collectively, they might be, in a sense, the sort of children described by Wordsworth in his "Ode," although that poet's romantic nature inclined him to believe that all children were the possessors of exceptional capacity for understanding the mysteries of man and nature. In some works of literature, children are deliberately described as precocious by the authors who create them. The youngsters are endowed with special powers about which the authors emphatically inform their readers. In D. H. Lawrence's short story, "The Rocking Horse Winner," a little boy named Paul is one such visionary, and another prophetic child occurs in Thomas Hardy's novel, *Jude the Obscure*. Both of these children are representative of the sacrifices society makes when its values are in the turmoil of change. Both of these children also possess a frightening inner wisdom about the changes and conflicts of their respective societies. Their author's social criticism is represented through them to a great extent. Much of the same thing might also be said for the children and adolescents created by J. D. Salinger. Certainly, the Glass family is populated by youngsters of exceedingly keen perception and extraordinary intelligence. Through them, their author is able to express certain philosophical values, much of which concerns the structure of the society in which the children live, and equally as much concerns all of mankind in relation to itself. In *Nine Stories*, Salinger's portrayal of children outside the Glass family is equally marked by heavy philosophical inquiry. One of the most familiar of all Salinger's characters is Holden Caulfield, the adolescent protagonist of *The Catcher in the Rye*. Maladjusted though he may appear to be, his interpretation of his society is only as distorted as that of any supersensitive teen-ager beset with problems with which he cannot cope. Despite the distortions of his concept, there is a validity to his attitude, for his alienation from both the world of his childhood and the world of adults makes him the artistic representation of a classic adolescent misfit. William Golding's novel, *Lord of the Flies*, utilizes children in still a different way. Not because they are exceptional or precocious boys, but because they represent so-called "normal" children whose knowledge and experience are limited by the age factor, the author develops around them an unusual set of circumstances in which no adults are included. In the absence of either the authority of the seeming wordly corruption of adults, these youngsters regress from civilized children to little savages, proving what according to the author is the inherent evil in mankind. Some of these isolated children instinctively realize what has happened to their values, and their attempts to deal with their problems might qualify them as precocious insofar as their fundamental but limited understanding is concerned.

ANNE FRANK'S POSITION

What place in the literature about children and their problems can be found for Anne Frank? We know, first of all, that *The Diary of a Young Girl* is not fiction, nor is it an artistically constructed memoir of someone's past. Neither is it the work of a professional writer. On the other hand, it is not merely the simple confessions of a teenage girl. While it serves as a document of World War II, it is not a journalistic account of battles or war strategy that might have been the work of a correspondent. Nor is it the sort of formal public testimony brought forth at the Nuremberg Trials after the war. In the strictest sense, Anne's work is not any of these things, and yet there are aspects of it that relate to all of them. It is a work of both the imagination and fact. Because it is a diary, we might best give it the synonym of a self-portrait.

With this as a working definition, our first consideration, as with any self-portrait, will be to know that we are seeing a self-interpretation of the creator. Because, in this case, she is young, she is apt to see herself both factually and fancifully. All the elements of her life thus become incorporated into the portrait; her family, her immediate associates, the war, the temper of the times. Because Anne is young, we will sympathize with her problems of growing up. We will understand that because of her age there are occasional distortions in her perspective. Her discoveries about life may be things we already know. Where she is naive, we may chuckle, because of our sophistication. Where she becomes profound in her observations of humanity, we may be astonished at her wisdom. In the analysis of herself and others, she may be harsh at times and awkward at others. Because this work is a diary, it concentrates on the little details of daily life, and in Anne's case, it is an unusually limited routine because of the confinements of the Frank's hiding place. But because Anne is an imaginative young person, she is able to delve deeply into a seemingly small environment and broaden its confines with a richness of detail that goes beyond the scope of the ordinary observer. These are the elements which combine to produce a portrait of great depth and dimension, further enhanced by the fact that a time span of two years went into the writing. Thus, the Diary reveals the development of its author but does not distract from the immediacy of what is communicated on each page.

A NOTE ON STYLE

Many aspects come into the consideration of an author's style. What the world "style" itself means is a combination of such features of writing as choice of words, figures of speech, sentence structure, rhythm patterns, and devices of language employed to produce certain effects. As authors gain personal maturity and experience in writing, their style goes through stages of development, arriving finally at one their readers recognize almost as a trademark. Most writers consciously work through many variations until they reach a leveling off into what remains essentially their own style. In other words, a method of expression is achieved consciously by a writer, even though his eventual style may or may not seem to the reader the obviously developed product of deliberate experimentation. Aside from style, an author's point of view is likely to alter with maturity. For better or for worse, depending on the circumstances of the writer's life, a development in thinking as well as manner of presentation results from experience. What bearing do these factors of style and content have on a reading of *The Diary of a Young Girl*?

The first necessary consideration is the author's age. Anne Frank was thirteen when she made the first entry in her diary and fifteen when she wrote the last. An unpracticed writer, save for training in composition at school, the diary, as she saw it, was simply a means of unburdening her innermost thoughts to an imaginary companion named Kitty. Of course, Kitty was the sort of friend who would have the most sympathetic response to Anne-an ideal confidant whose patience and understanding were guaranteed. Because there could be no opposition from Kitty to Anne's thoughts, the young writer could give voice to her most honest self in unthreatened privacy. Therefore, Anne could also experiment within her written expression. Beginning, naturally, with a style familiar to her from the classroom, the first entries are formally composed and somewhat self-conscious of their labored correctness. As the diary progresses, Anne seems to have fallen into an easier, more conversational style, identifiable by better turned but less rigidly constructed sentences. There is also a frequent easing into casual language. Besides style, the content develops as well throughout the pages. The author loses her inhibitions, unmasking more and more facets of her personality. The process is clearly one of self-discovery developing through the honest expression of her thoughts. The range is what might be expected from a girl of Anne's age-doubt, introspection, criticism, analysis, observation, – all directed to the purpose of getting to know herself.

Despite the fact that both the style and content show the development of Anne's maturity throughout the diary, there is a general lack of certain artificial touches used by older authors to screen their true characters from the reading public. Anne's straightforward expression is in evidence continually as she writes of matters both within herself and without. Sensitive to all things, she endows each entry with intensely personal and human expression, that manner of writing so like the self's own voice which many accomplished professional writers strive for but often fail to achieve. What also bears consideration is the great potential Anne's work reveals. For, had she lived to continue with her writing, it seems fairly safe to assume that she might have been successful as a professional writer. Such characteristics as her ability to detach herself as an observer, her skill in recording both the scenes of her external life, and the complexities with herself indicate the presence of remarkable talent. Her philosophical comments and injections of humor contribute to the high appraisal placed on her work. Who knows the extent of anyone's greatness without the help of time? Unfortunately, this was not a grant fate made to Anne. Readers must content themselves with the unfulfilled promise of her potential.

ANNE FRANK AND HISTORY

"I believe in the good of man," wrote a young girl in her diary, a girl experiencing the dehumanizing effects of a man whose slogan was, "My mission is to destroy and exterminate." The girl was a young Jewess named Anne Frank; the man tormenting her and her people was a dictator named Adolf Hitler. He succeeded in his mission to a great extent, but lost his cause in its entirety. His failure is the recorded history of World War II, and one document in its myriad testimony is *The Diary of a Young Girl*. The "Fuehrer" and the young girl were unequally matched in a contest of good and evil. History tells us that other such unequally matched conflicts have been resolved against the odds. An early lesson along these lines is the story of David and Goliath. Less immediately successful was the Maid of Orleans, known as Joan of Arc. Where she did not prevail in the physical battle against her adversaries, hers was an ultimate spiritual victory. Much the same can be said of Anne Frank, although her intentions and tactics were far different from those of the French girl. While Anne quietly penned in a private diary her spiritual crusade against the machinery of evil that in time destroyed her life and that of six million other Jews, her words have survived. As a document of World War II, her diary has helped bring judgment against the Nazi persecutors of Hitler's machine. As a work of literature, it has brought renewed inspiration to those who survived the Third Reich's atrocities. Moreover, the little journal has kept alive the spirit of an exceptional young person whose thoughts have broadened the perspective of millions of readers of all ages. Transcending nationality, race, and religion, *The Diary of a Young Girl* has been published in over twenty countries throughout the world. From its humble origins, it has become a monument to the nobility of the human spirit, a continuing affirmation of mankind's destiny to survive, and the exquisite triumph of good over evil.

THE DIARY OF A YOUNG GIRL

JUNE 14, 1942–JULY 9, 1942: LIFE ON THE OUTSIDE

Of the many gifts Anne Frank receives for her thirteenth birthday, the one she values most is a diary. Longing for the sort of friend with whom she can share everything, Anne names the diary "Kitty," declaring that the entries into the diary will be in the form of letters to her newly-created confidante. Anne's purpose in writing these letters is more than just that of reporting day-to-day occurrences. His intention is to reveal herself totally, unburdening all her thoughts as well as discussing her experiences at length.

Having stated her purpose in keeping the diary, Anne sketches briefly her autobiography. She tells Kitty how her family-father, mother and older sister Margot-came to Holland in 1933 from Germany to escape the early persecution of the Jews under Hitler. All went very pleasantly until 1940 when the Nazis invaded and conquered the Netherlands. Under Nazi occupation, the situation of the Jews even in Holland has grown increasingly unpleasant because of the anti-Jewish laws imposed by Hitler. Jews are banned from all modes of public and private transportation (except ferry boats), forbidden to attend all places of public entertainment, and prohibited from participation in all public sports. Jews are permitted to shop only in specially designated stores and then only at prescribed hours. Jews must attend special schools, be inside their homes by 8:00 P.M., and must wear the mark of their religion-a yellow six-pointed star known as a Star of David-displayed prominently on their person at all times.

In spite of these restrictions, Anne finds pleasure in life through relationships with her friends, reading, playing ping-pong, and in the security of her family. At the Jewish Secondary School which Anne and Margot have attended since required to withdraw from the Montessori School, there is great excitement over who will move up to the next form after the examinations. Anne comments to Kitty on the eccentricities of teachers and the intelligence or lack of it among her schoolmates. She describes her own bad habit of being a chatterbox for which she has been reprimanded at school. Anne also discusses her boy friends and her flirtatious nature, describing with pleasure the ups and downs of popularity among the opposite sex. Her best girl friends are schoolmates Lies Goosens and Jopie de Waal. She secretly favors Peter Wessel among the boys, but receives more attention from others, notably a lad of sixteen named Harry Goldberg. Harry is an immigrant from Belgium and lives with his grandparents who object to his seeing so much of a girl Anne's age. Nevertheless, Harry is well received at the Frank's home and despite his youthful seriousness, Anne admits that while she enjoys his attentions and his company, she is not in love with him. Anne also writes with nostalgia of "Granny," Mrs. Frank's mother, who came to live with the family in 1938 and who died in 1942.

BRIGHT NOTES STUDY GUIDE

Anne learns from her father that there are plans afoot for the family to go into hiding. For over a year the Franks have been distributing their possessions among Christian friends to avoid having them seized by the Germans. Recently Mr. Frank has withdrawn from active participation in his business, leaving in charge two trusted associates, Mr. Kraler and Mr. Koophuis. In recent weeks the S.S. (Secret Police) have been issuing more frequent "call-ups" for many Jews, which result in arrest and deportation. Because it is no longer possible either to leave Holland or to remain safely in their present mode of life, the only alternative for the Franks is to go into hiding. Plans and preparations have been made for this eventuality by the Franks and another family, the Van Daans. Aided by close friends who are also business associates, a "disappearance" has been arranged and a hiding place prepared. Aside from Kraler and Koophuis, the collaborators in the plan are Miep and Henk Van Santen, and Elli Vossen, a secretary. A call-up for Margot triggers the disappearance of the Franks a week ahead of schedule. With dizzying swiftness, the family is evacuated from their home in a matter of hours.

Once things have calmed down enough to permit Anne time to write in her diary, she describes the evacuation procedures to Kitty. From the moment of the call-up for Margot, the Frank household began proceeding with emergency measures. Throughout the day and much of the night, Miep and Henk made several trips from the Franks' house to the hiding place. On each trip, their pockets and satchels were crammed full of the Franks' possessions-such small articles of personal effects, food, and clothing as could be transported without arousing too much curiosity. The Franks themselves had hardly any sleep, arising at 5:30 A.M. and leaving things in a disarray two hours later.

JULY 11, 1942–JUNE 15, 1943: THE FIRST YEAR

For Anne, the beginning of their new life seems more like a vacation at a strange inn where the guests live in a nervous atmosphere of odd silence and necessary but peculiar rules. During the day all must be quiet so that no one employed downstairs or in the neighboring buildings will suspect their presence. Curtains, crudely made by Anne and Mr. Frank, now cover the windows and will never be taken down until the period of hiding is over. Minor decorations adorn the walls in an attempt to make the place seem more cheerful. Nevertheless, Anne finds the silence very frightening, and even more oppressive is the notion that she can never go outdoors. The fear of discovery underlies every action and is a constant source of tension.

Within three days, the Van Daan family arrives-husband, wife, sixteen-year-old son Peter, and Mouschi, the cat. The Franks are relieved to learn that everyone on the outside has a different theory regarding their own disappearance. Even Mr. Goudsmit, a lodger in the Frank's former home, has been successfully tricked into thinking that they have escaped to Switzerland. It does not take long, however, for the seven inhabitants to develop little tensions, first within their own families and then between members of the other group. Mrs. Frank and Mrs. Van Daan early develop a petty rivalry over utensils and other communal household supplies. Anne finds herself easily upset by her own mother and the Van Daans, except for Peter who manages to stay out of everyone's way. Mr. and Mrs. Van Daan quarrel in such a way that Franks find it both appalling and amusing. Anne begins to recognize the difference in the standards and values of the two families and the difficulties of adjustment. As the realities of their confinement become more apparent through the limited routine of daily life, so do each person's selfish tendencies. Bickering and tears are not uncommon.

Although Anne has taken a holiday from studies until September, she and the others read a great deal to occupy their time. Mr. Koophuis brings new books each Saturday. Some are considered too adult for Anne and Peter at this time, and incidents regarding forbidden reading matter occur as a result. Aside from household duties, an activity shared by all is listening to the radio downstairs in the private office in the evening when no one is about. Although it is illegal to have the dial turned to any station other than Germany, the group listens only to broadcasts of music on that station, for other Nazi programs are too hateful and depressing. They prefer the newscasts and other programs of the BBC (English) which are more encouraging. Queen Wilhelmina of the Netherlands often sends messages to her subjects over the airwaves from England where she and her family are in exile. The occupants also take heart from Winston Churchill's speeches.

The families receive their food and other supplies from their protectors, Miep, Henk, Elli, and Messrs. Kraler and Koophuis. They have been able to purchase extra ration books on the black market and their food supply is adequate at present. An added security measure is the building of a sliding cupboard in front of the doorway leading to the hidden apartment. Through this disguised doorway come their allies on visits, bringing supplies as well as news and encouragement. Except for the footsteps of these trusted friends, other noises in the building at the wrong hours bring terror to the hearts of all. One such incident occurs when Koophuis' rapping on the door is thought to be that of a workman who has come to fix the fire extinguishers. The three days during which a plumber is making repairs are also anxious ones, as no water facilities may be used nor may there be any activity at all during his working hours downstairs. One particularly tense moment comes with the inspection of the building by a new owner of whose purchase no one was notified.

Koophuis is obliged to show him the premises and does so. He pretends to have forgotten the key to the doorway leading to the secret portion in back of the Private Office. Fortunately, he is not questioned by the new owner.

An eighth person is added to the group, Albert Dussel, whose wife has already left the country. Anne has her reservations about sharing a room with the elderly dentist, but such arrangements are not ones of choice. Dussel is amazed at the elaborate system of living accommodations in the hiding place. Although their protectors have held back many of the ugly details of life on the outside, the group's curiosity is so persistent that Dussel reveals many of the sad and alarming Nazi activities which have taken place since the group has taken up residence in hiding. Particularly depressing are the reports of Jews being deported and sent to their deaths, many of whom were friends and acquaintances of the occupants. Mr. Dussel, in turn, is rather stunned by the quarrels which seem never to cease among those in the hideout. He attempts to ignore the tension by pursuing his own interests and projects.

Anne writes extensively about the personality conflicts, many of which involve her in one way or another. She is thought to be quite spoiled by her parents according to the Van Daans and Dussel. She and her mother are constantly on bad terms. Margot and Anne also have their differences. The result is usually that Anne seeks justification from her father whose method of arbitration is one of judicious sympathy for Anne coupled with a more gentle explanation of her faults rather than a severe reprimand. Mr. Frank will not become too strong an ally of anyone in these battles. Mrs. Van Daan and Mrs. Frank have growing tensions, not only from conflicts over communal supplies and differing values, but also because Mrs. Van Daan attempts to flirt with both Mr. Frank and Mr. Dussel. Anne and Mrs. Van Daan do not always get on well, for the older woman's disapproval of the girl's upbringing is one of her favorite topics. This often brings the Van Daans and the Franks into larger disagreements. Mr. and Mrs. Van Daan quarrel regularly in unpleasant terms and tones of voice. Mr. Dussel has his irritating little ways, one of which is siding with Anne's critics. Arbitration in most of these matters comes from Mr. Frank.

In spite of these difficulties, the eight have other activities which help the time pass. Reading, of course, is a favorite. Lessons have begun, and Anne is studying English, Dutch, French, history, mathematics, and shorthand. She is interested as well in Greek and Roman mythology and art history. The women attend to the household chores and the men do their share in maintaining security and making certain repairs. Each has one or more personal pastimes. Anne's hobby is collecting pictures of film stars and reading articles about the cinema. For Mr. Frank, it is translating Dickens into English and reading classical German plays aloud to the group. All listen attentively to the shortwave radio, but now the large receiver downstairs has been turned over to the authorities on demand and has been replaced by an illegal "baby" set upstairs. News and other broadcasts are always material for extended discussions. The grownups recount stories of their youth. Riddles are asked all around. Some participate in practicing conversational foreign languages. The women do needlework. A regular part of the routine is sitting up exercises since there is no other opportunity for physical sports. Each person's birthday merits a celebration usually highlighted by whatever delicacies of food, flowers, or other merchandise that their protectors can procure on the market, where prices are soaring. Holidays, both Christian and Jewish, such as Chanukah, St. Nicholas' Day, Christmas, Whitsunday, and Easter are pleasant breaks in the monotony.

Despite their insular existence, the eight occupants of the secret apartment are not untouched by the events of the outside world. The war news affects one and all. Eagerly they await their liberation in the form of an invasion by the Allies. The bombing of nearby German towns and air battles overhead keep them awake trembling with fear at night. The plight of the Jews sickens them, for cautious peeks through the curtains reveal lorries rolling along the streets filled with the persecuted on their way to concentration camps. Children in rags are begging in the streets, adult faces are grim. Many young Dutchmen are being sent to German labor camps. The Nazis play havoc with currency and ration books, causing even more consternation. Clothing that is outgrown or becomes too tattered is extremely difficult to replace. When one of their protectors becomes ill, a great handicap is created and the others must work overtime. There is always the possibility and occasionally the reality of burglars breaking into the warehouse below. Fortunately, the hidden rooms remain undiscovered by the house breakers.

Anne reflects on the conditions of life in the outside world. She is horrified at the grim aspect of Amsterdam life which she perceives in those occasional peeks through the curtains. Overcome by pity for the urchins begging in the streets she wishes she might bring them upstairs for at least a good washing. Her conscience pricks her when she thinks of the relative safety and comfort of her existence compared to the wretched plight of the many Jews and others being sent to their deaths. Tales of the concentration camps and the atrocities committed by the Nazis before the inmates are gassed are so awful to Anne that she must force herself not to dwell on those thoughts. Reports of resistance measures taken by the Dutch people are encouraging at first but eventually depressing, for the Nazis so quickly crush such actions and as punishment make conditions worse than before. How much she and the others despise the Fuehrer! Anne comments bitterly on the sort of German citizen created by Hitler and is thankful that although she was born a German she no longer qualifies as one since Hitler has denationalized all Jews. She eagerly awaits the day when she can acquire Dutch citizenship and vows to go to any length to achieve this goal, even if it means personally confronting Queen Wilhelmina. Despite the depressing awareness of the war outside their safe hiding place, Anne vows to keep up her spirits. She will force the dreadful thoughts out of her mind, for only in this way can she find a reason to believe in going on.

Looking inward, Anne often comments on how alone she feels. She realizes that she is set apart from the values and ideas of the grownups. She longs to be respected for her own opinions, rather than censured for what they consider juvenile behavior or impudence. She is also quite generous with her own criticisms of the others in the diary. She writes to Kitty mournfully of her alienation from her mother who, she feels, is not all a mother should be. Her father is her ideal, but, in many ways unreachable. Margot and she are too vastly different in temperament and outlook to be close friends. She resents the apparent preference of the others for her older sister. Peter lives in a shell and isn't that interesting so far. Mr. Dussel's slowness to understand things irritate. Anne, and his impatience with her is another sore point. Anne lacks respect for Mrs. Van Daan's intelligence and finds her selfish and immodest in many ways. Anne feels herself the object of everyone's criticism. Each day she vows to overcome her faults, yet she is intent upon remaining a distinct individual. Such conflicts are often the subject of many letters to Kitty.

JULY 11, 1943–AUGUST 1, 1944: THE SECOND YEAR

After a year together, the eight occupants are accustomed to the hazards both from within and from without. There area still the flare-ups between personalities, the rapidly decreasing availability of goods and supplies. The air raids are nerve-wracking and the war news affects their morale almost more than anything else. Illness visits each of the inhabitants by turns in the form of colds or flu. No medical help is available, so they must use whatever home remedies and their limited supply of drugs will permit. It is difficult to avoid contagion and impossible not to be an inconvenience to everyone else when illness strikes. Anne's eyes have grown so bad and her headaches so frequent and severe that the possibility of her going outside to an oculist is seriously considered, but not realized because the risk is too great. The weather causes more discomfort, particularly the summer heat because the windows must remain closed and curtained. The desire to go outdoors frustrates everyone, particularly the younger ones. Keeping hope alive is a goal in itself for each and all.

To make the passage of time more bearable for the young people, Mr. Frank steps up the intellectual activity. For Margot, there is a correspondence course in Latin which she takes in Elli's name. Peter works harder at French. Anne and her sister are given some routine clerical work to do for the business. Anne's interest in genealogical tables is encouraged, and her father helps her work out the lineage of many European royal families.

As a precautionary measure, many pounds of dried peas and beans as well as tins of other foodstuffs were stored away before the group took up residence. Now some of the dried beans are

BRIGHT NOTES STUDY GUIDE

spoiling, so there is a new project for everyone. Bean rubbing, to remove the mold which has formed on the bean skins, is an activity which keeps at least part of the self-occupied and aids the passage of time. Then, too, when the produce market is flooded with a certain commodity, the price is lowered and the occupants have that item purchased by their protectors in large quantities. When such amounts are delivered, all hands must set to work. Strawberries, for instance, must be prepared for jam, syrup, and canning whole. Similarly, the shelling and preserving of peas requires a portion of everyone's time. But the novelty of such projects soon wanes, leaving everyone bored and somewhat sickened with peas and strawberries which will have to be eaten nevertheless.

Food presents other problems, too. When ration shortages occur it is likely that only one or two foods will appear at all meals for several days or even weeks. Such items as lettuce, potatoes, kale or spinach prepared in a variety of ways but served exclusively can result in disagreeable stomachs and dispositions. Table manners reflect the condition of current rations. Often conversations are simply extended wishful thoughts about which foods each person misses and longs for. As often as possible, Miep and Elli find a treat of some delicacy for the group, most often at holiday time or for someone's birthday.

Aside from individual worries are other problems arising from such incidents as Mouschi's fleas which infect the living quarters for a short time. Maintaining the physical security of the premises is of major importance as burglars twice break into the warehouse. Repairs must be made immediately and the men are preoccupied with their tours of inspection and guard duty. Most fearsome are the air raids. Each occupant has prepared an "escape bag" in the event that an evacuation becomes necessary. But the problem in such a case is contradictory, for to leave the hideout would be as dangerous as remaining in a bombed building. Many discussions center around the better alternative, but no decision can be agreed upon by all. Another favorite pastime of the adults is a political discussion after each radio broadcast. Often they are divided into two groups, the optimists and the pessimists. The discussions eventually lead to the same subject; who will win the war? There is standard speculation about the war's outcome and the strategy of each country. The most feverish item of debate is the forthcoming Allied invasion. When it occurs on June 6, 1944, hopes soar for a speedy liberation. But always they go back to the wistful questions of how soon and under what circumstances the war will end. Such discussions often become unpleasantly heated.

Other news of the outside reaches them from their protectors. The activities of the Dutch underground movement are of great interest. Although much information is encouraging, some incidents are cause for alarm. Their vegetable grocer is arrested for concealing Jews. Others involved in resistance are also punished by the Nazis. Anne is overcome with appreciation for the risks their own protectors take without voicing fear or complaints. The strain, however, tells on their helpers. Mr. Koophuis has recurrent hemorrhages from a stomach ulcer and must be hospitalized. Elli's nerves are wearing thin from concerns over her sick father, her fiance who has been sent to do forced labor in Germany, her routine office work, and her additional duties for the eight occupants. Miep and Henk have occasional illnesses which keep either one or both from helping their Jewish friends. Mr. Kraler receives a call-up to put in four weeks of forced labor. Then, too, one of the warehousemen is thought to be untrustworthy and displays curiosity about the upper floors. He must be carefully handled to curb his suspicions.

The second year is marked for Anne less by these events which, although meaningful, are not so fascinating as the alterations in her relationships with the others and those signs of her own mental and physical maturity. Looking back on her entries over the past year, she is rather surprised at some of the fury released on the pages. Although there are still personality conflicts among them all, Anne feels that she has learned to handle herself better, and thus not cause such criticism to be showered upon her. Too, she recognizes that living in such confinement compounded by the strain and tension of war causes problems among people, which might otherwise never occur. Therefore, she looks for good things in others, and tries to ignore the bad. Anne is aware, however, that her relationship with her mother will never match the closeness between Margot and Mrs. Frank. Accepting this fact, she becomes more adept at not hurting her mother to the degree she has in the past. Another outgrowth of her maturity is a new, if not complete, friendship with her sister. They can share much, but not everything. Sadly, Anne also recognizes the ways in which she has grown away from her father and how, even from him, she has withheld parts of herself. These realizations increase her loneliness and feed her hunger for a friend. Her diary isn't the same as a real human being. Accompanying her longing for a companion with whom she can share mutual trust and understanding, she dreams intensely of her old friends, Lies Goosens and Peter Wessel.

One morning she awakes from a particularly vivid dream of Peter Wessel and that day seeks to initiate a friendship with Peter Van Daan, whom until now, she has all but ignored. Peter is shy and reserved, but Anne is patient and persistent. Little by little, during the last half of the second year, the two form a relationship which develops from friendship into a tender young romance. Made aware of the dangers of unrestrained involvement by their parents, the relationship is controlled by both Anne and Peter. They spend long hours together sharing confidences, ambitions, and fears. Vowing never to argue as they have seen their elders do so unpleasantly, the girl, now fifteen, and the boy, just past seventeen, work out their problems in long, patient conversations. Anne soon realizes, however, that she is not in love with Peter, even though she has allowed him to give her the first kiss of her life. She is too aware of certain flaws in his character to commit herself to the thought of a future with him until she has seen how he grows up. She also grows to realize that although she has given her life an object when she needed it, Peter is much more dependent on her than she on him. This is disconcerting, for Anne has simultaneously discovered the greater need for self-reliance. She believes that with confidence and maturity, Peter will acquire this independence too, and that perhaps she can help him toward this goal.

As important to Anne as her relationship with Peter is her relationship to herself. In this area, the seeds of self-knowledge have been sown, and blossoming forth are a philosophy of life, a scale of values, a set of ideals, and a developing ambition for her future as an adult. Anne is aware of herself as an individual with a set of values apart from those of her parents. Firm in her opinions, she contemplates her own behavior, that of the grownups, and the actions of all mankind. Reflecting primarily on the conditions caused by the war, she remarks how senselessly cruel and futile war itself is. Fear and depression fostered by events outside and the confining conditions inside are combatted by the lectures Anne gives herself to maintain courage, hope, and faith in God. Her spirits again revived, Anne considers her love of nature as a great source of consolation. Another uplifting thought is her newly realized ambition to be either a journalist, or a writer. In addition to the entries in her diary, she has written a few short stories. After the war, she hopes to publish a book called *Het Achterhuis (The House In The Back)* using her diary as a guide.

Summarizing herself as a "little bundle of contradictions," she discusses the lighthearted, seemingly superficial Anne which she displays to the world. In contrast, she writes of the deeper, finer Anne, who is too shy to reveal herself to the others. Always questioning life's meaning, Anne explores the value of life versus death. Still searching, questioning, and answering, Anne makes a typical entry on Tuesday, August 1, 1944. Unknowingly, she has written the last.

COMMENTARY

June 14, 1942–July 9, 1942: Life On The Outside

Outlook

Because this is a diary, it is important to distinguish from the beginning those passages which tend to be more objective from those that are highly subjective. It is necessary also to be attuned to the moods of the writer which, considering her age and the circumstances of her life, fluctuate greatly and are reflected by variations in tone throughout the diary. Because Anne is in the process of growing up, there are apt to be contradictions in her thinking as she matures. By the same token, it is wise to look for those areas of her thinking which develop consistently. One must remember too that the work itself was not intended as a finished product for publication. The diary was considered by Anne as a confidante, an imaginary friend to whom she could confess her most private thoughts and release her deepest emotions. There is no attempt by the author to control the content of her entries. This fact is of the utmost importance to the reader whose perspective must be adjusted accordingly.

A New Friend

The beginning of the diary is comprised of entries which may be analogous to the beginning of any relationship. This is manifested in the form of informative passages concerning Anne's background and present situation. It is as if she is introducing herself to Kitty with warmth of expression but also with the natural reserve accorded a newly made friend. There is a note of cautious intimacy where Anne confides to Kitty her deep longing for the true friend she hopes the diary will prove to be. Remaining fairly objective in spite of due cause for bitterness, Anne describes the difficulties being encountered by her family and others who are victims of Hitler's anti-Jewish laws. Although the hardships and inconveniences make her wistful, she does not feel life to be unbearable. There are compensations, among them the attentions of her schoolmates. She rather boastfully describes her enjoyment of this popularity with somewhat of a devil-may-care attitude. This is something which Anne will look back upon later, and in reflection, it will be a signpost of her maturity.

Grownups

Anne's attitude toward the authority of grownups is revealed in this early in this early section by her comments on the "freakishness" of teachers. She is clever enough to amuse them even when she is being reprimanded. Because she can get off so lightly now, it is important to compare her later reactions to criticism and correction. Her independent spirit, even at this stage, is evident, and should be interesting to trace through the diary.

Boy Friends

It may seem at first peculiar to the reader that Anne has "boy friends" at her age. While these are not seriously romantic relationships, they are not considered the same as friendships with members of her own sex. Rather, they are indications of her general popularity and wholesome but thoroughly feminine nature. Anne's only real "crush" is on Peter Wessel, but this again differs from a serious, boy-girl attraction. It is another important item, because later on she will remember Peter Wessel and feel this early crush in a much more mature way. This is also an indicator of Anne's depth of feeling in its carry-over from girlhood to young womanhood.

Zionism

Anne mentions that Harry Goldberg, one of her current admirers, secretly attends meetings of the Zionist Movement, although his grandparents disapprove. Zionism was and still is a movement dedicated to the establishment of Palestine (now the State of Israel) as a homeland for the Jews. Harry's grandparents represent the Assimilationists, those opposed to Zionism on the grounds that it was more important for Jews to become integrated citizens of the countries in which they resided despite overt anti-Semitism in Europe. Hitler's persecution of the Jews did more to illuminate the pros and cons of Zionism than any other single factor in the twentieth century. Zionism itself can be traced back to the Old Testament from which much of the Movement's early theory was adapted. Margot, herself, is interested in Zionism as indicated by her desire to be a teacher in Palestine after finishing school.

Progressive Parents

Anne's mother and father might be considered quite "modern" with respect to their children's upbringing. They do not exert traditional sort of disciplinary pressure on their daughters as might be expected from European parents. The Frank's philosophy later becomes a subject of controversy, and even Anne indicates an ambivalent attitude toward it. The earliest evidence of the Frank's progressive methods is the way in which they treat their daughters' grades at school. Rather than stress the importance of excellent report cards, the Franks feel that the girls should be happy, healthy and polite, and the rest will take care of itself.

S. S. Call-Up

The Franks have good cause for terror when Margot receives the "call-up" from the S. S. It was not uncommon for the Nazis to take girls in their middle and late teens for the most unsavory purposes. Once a family member's name appeared on the call-up list, it was the end, not only for that particular individual, but for the entire family whose doom was guaranteed. Despite any temporary success achieved in buying someone's name off a Nazi list, the eventual call-up came anyway. Therefore, the Franks were prudent in disappearing immediately after the first one came for Margot.

Disappearance

Notice how the Franks have strived to preserve a normal existence until the last minute. Even their lodger, Mr. Goudsmit, is not aware of changes in the household. It must not be thought, however, that he and other uninvolved Dutch people were oblivious to the situation of the Jews. Many of those engaged neither in the underground movement nor the Dutch Nazi party simply "looked away" from all suspicious activities. To protect themselves, they remained "neutral," and while deliberately knowing nothing, could guess much. Theirs was not an enviable position, however, for they were suspected of knowledge by the Gestapo and distrusted as well by the underground. Consequently, these uninvolved persons frequently suffered mistreatment from both sides.

Reaction

Notice the different reactions of the members of the Frank family to the disappearance and first day in hiding. Because Anne is young it seems for her some sort of strange and romantic adventure. She is quite keyed up and only too eager to help her father with the work. Margot and Mrs. Frank, on the other hand, are depressed and physically affected by the move. They are not able to cope with the initial chaos. But their adjustment into the new life comes more easily than Anne's adjustment does once things are settled. It is not surprising that Mrs. Frank, accustomed to comfort and security, should be affected in this way. Perhaps Margot realizes less than her mother but more than her sister just what going into hiding means, and thus reacts in a manner similar to that of Mrs. Frank. Mr. Frank seems able to cope with most of the circumstances as they arise. Like Anne, he too has delayed reactions, but less pronounced than those of his younger daughter, naturally, because of his maturity.

Style

From the very first entry in the diary, we are impressed by Anne's ability to organize and synthesize material. This is indicated by the orderly presentation of facts, the lucid description of circumstances, and the limited use of unnecessary adjectives. While she is orderly and precise in her presentation of material, Anne does not overlook opportunities for personal comments and subtle indications of both her humorous and serious sides. Despite the tendency of young people to ramble on, once Anne has discussed something she moves on to another topic with a surprising lack of awkwardness in transition. Notice, too, the smooth insertions of dialog which subtly indicate the personality of the speaker in a way surprisingly compatible with Anne's descriptions of the person. This is important for subsequent character analysis, because it shows that although we see the characters from Anne's point of view, the very revealing nature of the dialog itself attests to the validity of the narrator's opinion.

THE DIARY OF A YOUNG GIRL

JULY 11, 1942–JUNE 15, 1943: THE FIRST YEAR

. . . .

QUARRELS

It should come as no surprise that the confinement of their existence and the overexposure to each other would cause sharp personality conflicts among the first seven occupants. It is said, and here it seems most aptly illustrated, that no house is big enough for two women. Mrs. Frank and Mrs. Van Daan lose no time in developing a rivalry which, although it may seem petty to the reader, is not a very strange thing at all. It appears that their disagreements stem mainly from such trifles as communal dishes or linens, but given more thought, one realizes that the two women have widely different standards and values. Mrs. Frank's social background is certainly one of a different social level from that of Mrs. Van Daan. Hence, their personalities find deeper areas of conflict than those which appear on the surface over mundane matters. Even their methods of combat are different. Whereas Mrs. Frank usually withdraws after an arch remark with her ruffled cloak of dignity wrapped about her, Mrs. Van Daan vents her emotions in a rather coarse barrage of angry words and frequent tears.

THE FRANKS' FAMILY PROBLEMS

Anne's youth manifests itself in continuous chattering and seemingly impudent laughter. With all the pent up energy of a thirteen-year old and none of the physical outlets she formerly enjoyed, it is no wonder she annoys her elders. Consequently, the only recourse of the others is to scold her or her parents, and thus the conflicts go round robin. Margot is more unassuming than her younger sister and seems to aggravate the others less, yet she too reacts, we are told by Anne, in the form of catty remarks and taking sides with her mother when Mrs. Frank and Anne have a flare-up. The relationship between Anne and her mother is strained because Anne obviously prefers her father to the exclusion of the other parent. Realizing this Mr. Frank is in an uncomfortable middle ground. However, he is wise enough to see Anne as passing through an "oedipal" phase, not uncommon for young girls in which they are "in love" with their fathers and develop a rivalry with their mothers. Hence, Mr. Frank does his best to give Anne the affection she craves, combining it with a fatherly authority and encouragement to better behavior rather than harsh reprimands. Loyal to his wife and older daughter, he is the veritable peacemaker of the family.

THE VAN DAAN'S FAMILY PROBLEMS

The Van Daans have other family problems. As husband and wife, their relationship differs from that of Mr. and Mrs. Frank. Anne has never heard her parents quarrel, and finds the Van

Daan's marital rows both upsetting and amusing. The Van Daans seem to expend a good deal of energy in these quarrels, but Anne notes the tenderness with which they eventually make up. Perhaps, she realizes, this is another kind of love between married people, and while different from that of her parents and not to her taste, it is love nevertheless. Peter, rather awkward and shy at this stage of his life, keeps pretty much to himself. Although the quarrels of his parents probably embarrass him, they are certainly no novelty. This does not mean that he is immune to either the bickering or the confinements of the life in hiding. At first, he has symptoms of imaginary physical ailments and his hypochondria is as valid a form of getting attention as Anne's chattering. Later we learn that Peter lets off steam by going up to the attic to swear. The only disciplinary incident in which he is notably involved concerns his clandestine reading of a forbidden book. Once again, it is Mr. Frank's duty as peacemaker to arbitrate between Mr. Van Daan and his son.

STRAIN OF CONFINEMENT

It is not only the confinement which causes a strain on everyone's nerves. Remember, these two families are locked away from the civilization that they have known. They have ceased to exist as far as the outside world is concerned. Their lives are in their own hands and those of their protectors. They have no function other than that of staying alive – and this at their own peril. They are helpless prisoners of time and fate. Surrounded by hostility from without, they have only each other to depend on and live for. All other concerns have been taken out of their lives. Marking time with no other ostensible function than continuing to live is a difficult exercise for human beings. Charged as they are with energy and emotion, it is small wonder that relationships are not worse. Living in constant fear of discovery, which means certain death, the seven must also cope with the immediacy of such a disaster. While everything that goes on in the outside world affects them, they are impotent insofar as being effective in return. Theirs is simply the task of enduring. Frustrated from within and without their quarters, these people have to cultivate what Mrs. Frank calls the "Art of Living." This means that seven individuals with distinct personal values and opinions must reorganize themselves into a different species of creature which exists far outside anything they have either imagined or experienced.

THE DIARY AS AN OUTLET

Anne retaliates for the reprimands she receives by "letting go" in her diary with comments that reveal fury, humor, and wisdom. At first, she writes a round of angry criticism aimed at whoever has happened to annoy her. She even gloats if these individuals have been beaten in some other fray. Then she reflects upon adult behavior in general, finding it far from flawless. She is perceptive enough to see that even though her elders have the advantage of age, and can condemn her with relative impunity, their shortcomings are no more tolerable than her own. How often children are able to see through the devices of adulthood! After she has released her anger, Anne pauses to consider herself. She attempts to rationalize the criticism she has received with certain justifications. As if holding up a mirror to herself she asks, "Am I really so bad?" After a few more blusters, she vows to outgrow her failings and to set such a good example that all will be forever silent in awe of her perfection. As she gradually cools off, Anne makes some humorous worldly-wise remark signifying that she is ready to sally forth again now that self-repairs have been made.

DAILY LIFE

Some of Anne's best descriptions are those concerning the little aspects of everyday living that a less observant and expressive person might overlook. The facts of life and nature's necessities are treated by Anne with surprising maturity and honesty. She manages to give even the greatest inconveniences caused by faulty plumbing or undigestable food a touch of humor, but is never offensive in this respect. Anne's curiosity and wholesomeness enable her to take a lesson about the external sex differences of cats from Peter Van Daan without batting an eye. Of course, Peter's open attitude is extremely helpful, too. Anne realizes here that some of her schoolyard whispers on such topics were ridiculous.

OTHER JEWS

Mournfully, Anne recounts to Kitty the gloomy stories of Jews being deported and sent from Holland to German concentration camps. She feels guilty for her own safe existence in comparison to the fate in store for others. It is almost more than she can bear when she thinks of her young friends being mistreated and killed. What a dreadful thing for any young girl to contemplate! But this is one of the realities of war with which all must cope. Her parents, too, know of their friends' deportations and deaths. Their protectors try very hard to keep such news from the Franks and Van Daans, but the radio is not choosy about its listeners. Anne is incredulous at the cruelty of the Gestapo and the innocence of their victims. Such periods of contemplation often result in hopeless tears followed by little pep talks in which she revives her courage and her faith. But there is no answer to why all this must be.

INTELLECTUAL ACTIVITY

Notice how eager Anne is for intellectual activity. This is not only the result of being deprived of other forms of amusement. Her wide range of serious interests are valid indicators of her basic intellectual curiosity. The reports in her diary of translating books from other languages show her verbal proficiency. Admittedly, she dislikes all forms of mathematics, but does not seem either unable or unwilling to do her assignments. (It is not uncommon for those with high verbal aptitude to have significantly lower potential for mathematics.) Mr. Frank is a great source of intellectual stimulation for Anne. Realizing the needs of his daughter's keen and curious mind, he seeks new ways for her to exercise her mental power, giving much of his own time to partake in these endeavors with her. Often Anne remarks that as soon as the war is over she can return to her studies at school, but she seems to be doing an excellent job of keeping up on her own in the meantime.

RATIONING

During the war, there was a world-wide shortage of consumer products. This was caused by the diversion of many raw materials into war goods. It was also caused by the impossibility of transporting materials through customary land, sea, and air channels now blocked by hostile forces. As supplies were limited, governments (including that of the United States) issued to their citizens ration books containing coupons for different types of commodities. These included food and any article made from materials being converted to war use, such as rubber, nylon, petroleum, and leather. Ration books were intended to limit the quantity of available supplies and to provide equal distribution among the populace. It was possible in some instances to procure extra ration books by illegal means. (The Franks had four such illegal books.) It was also possible, but far too costly for the average person, to procure rationed articles on what is termed the "black market." This expression stands for the buying and selling of rationed materials outside legal channels. Because this sort of trading was conducted beyond the law, the costs of goods on the black market was excessive. Such profiteering was not uncommon in all countries, and black marketeers were somewhat despised.

HOLIDAYS

Familiar to most readers are the Christian holidays. Christmas and Easter and the Jewish holiday, Chanukah. Less familiar, probably because they are not as widely celebrated in the United States, are the Christian holidays, Whitsunday and St. Nicholas Day. The seventh Sunday after Easter is known as Whitsunday, commemorating the descent of the Holy Ghost. Another religious idea connected with Whitsunday is that on this day the Apostles were filled with wisdom (wit) by the Holy Ghost. St. Nicholas day occurs on December 6th and commemorates one of the most popular saints in Christendom. Said to have been Bishop of Myra in the 4th century, he has become the patron saint of Russia, Aberdeen (Scotland), scholars, pawnbrokers, little boys, and parish clerks. There are many legends connected with St. Nicholas which explain his multiple patronage. He is also the original figure upon whom Santa Claus is based. Although the occupants of the hiding place are Jewish, they celebrate these Christian holidays for the first time while in hiding, more to relieve the tedium than for religious or social reasons. Yet they show as much respect for these unaccustomed Christian festivals as for their own Jewish holidays.

JEWISH IDENTITY

Anne's sense of being Jewish is rather an interesting one. Made aware of her religion from an early age, it has been less from a sense of piety but more from an awareness of belonging to a separate group that has cultivated Anne's identity as a Jewess. She reflects much on the Jews versus the Germans, stating with precocious insight that the two groups are the "greatest enemies in the world." Behind Anne's sense of identity is an historical pattern of anti-Semitism and Jewish segregation in Europe. Even the wealthy, cultured, upper-middle-class background from which Anne's family comes has not been beyond prejudicial treatment. Those Jews permitted educational and social privileges, possessing the advantages of wealth and culture, were never fully accepted into the fabric of society in the nations where they resided. The history of the Jews is one of tightly contained group living for protection against the inevitability of anti-Semitism and eventual expulsion. Anne is part of this traditional pattern of European Jewry. Therefore, she is able to accept with a surprising degree of tolerance the initial anti-Semitic legislation and the early hardships. Her comments regarding the progressively harsher treatment of the Jews reflect more horror and pity than bitterness, more outrage against persecution in general. Then, too, from her protected though risky position in hiding, she has lost the fullest sense of identification. Thus set apart, she can view with objectivity the plight of the Jews, and while she might feel guilty about her safety and comfort, she is less apt to feel the extremes of personal bitterness that more direct contact would have created. Anne's position, then, must be understood in its complexity as that of: 1) inherently aware of her separate identity as a Jew; 2) victimized by Hitler's persecution of the Jews; 3) as a temporary bystander whose suspended participation enables her to view things with more objective sympathy.

Contrast Anne's attitude toward her Jewish identification with that of Peter or Margot. Peter is decidedly bitter and resentful about being a Jew. He contemplates converting to Christianity after the war. Anne finds this a distressing idea, and tries to convince him that he will always be a Jew because of his birth, and if he comes through the trials of Hitler's persecution, there will be no need to convert anyway. Margot, on the other hand, strongly identifies with her Jewish heritage, and although not clearly stated in Anne's diary, it seems fairly reasonable to assume that she has Zionist leanings. Although secretive about her plans for the future, she indicates a desire to teach or do other work in Palestine. Anne tends to be more of an Assimilationist. Intent on retaining her identity as a Jewess, she would nevertheless prefer to become a full-fledged Dutch citizen after the war.

POLITICS

Although much of Anne's political opinion is formed by the attitude of the grownups, she is independent enough in her thinking and expression to comment astutely and with a degree of sophisticated humor on many public personalities and war developments. Notice her utter contempt and disgust for Hitler and her ability to see through many of his propaganda tactics. Many of her remarks indicate a wisdom of such matters beyond her years. For instance, when the others are selfishly impatient for the Allied invasion to begin, Anne explains in her diary how much more important it is for the English to defend their own territory and employ aggression on other battlefronts despite the anxiety of the Dutch under German occupation. How needlessly, according to Anne, the grownups frustrate each other with constant speculation and debate over political affairs. She realizes, too, how important these events are to their welfare, not only in terms of ultimate liberation but also for providing conversational material, even if the result is a quarrel. Notice the familiarity with which she speaks of Winston Churchill, Dwight D. Eisenhower, and others who now figure as legends in the history of World War II. A look at the memoirs of these men might be helpful in rounding out the reader's perspective.

EFFECTS OF WAR

Consider the stamina of these people under the strain of confined quarters, short rations, the threat of discovery-all compounded by the nerve-wracking conditions created by air raids. The bombing of nearby German towns can be plainly heard. The Nazi antiaircraft guns based in Holland open fire regularly. Air battles take place overhead between the Allies and Nazis, creating the possibility of unintended but imminent disaster for the Dutch below. No wonder Anne and the others react with trembling, tears, upset stomachs, and other nervous effects. But all they can do is hope and pray that their building will not be hit. Their "escape bags," as Anne pointed out, are just psychological devices for the sake of having something to hold on to. Only too well do they know that leaving their hideout would be as lethal as having a bomb come through the roof. Mrs. Van Daan's hysterics are a source of amusement and pity for Anne depending on how badly she herself is affected. Notice Anne's continual attempts to be stoical under such circumstances and how annoyed with herself she becomes when she reacts with uncontrollable fear. Many seasoned soldiers returned from the war with symptoms of shell shock from just such conditions as those experienced by the eight in hiding. It is noteworthy, then, how really strong these people were in resisting severe nervous disorders under the hazards of noise, shock, and knowledge of their defenselessness.

GROWING PAINS

As the first year in hiding draws to an end, we can look back on Anne's entries in her diary and see significant areas of development in her maturity. Not unique among persons her age are the "growing pains" which signify the end of childhood and the beginning of adulthood. This uncomfortable period of adolescence is the subject of many articles and books familiar to contemporary readers as popular interest in psychology grows each year. At the time of Anne's writing, however, the subject of adolescent problems was not as highly publicized as it is now. Nor were Europeans, generally speaking, as predisposed to the ventilation of such topics as Americans. The traditional European attitude toward young people is reflected in the comments of Dussel and the Van Daans who find the flexibility of the Franks with respect to their daughters' upbringing rather shocking and much too "modern." The Franks seem more "progressive," and certainly more like American parents in their broad-minded attitude and permissiveness. Anne, however, resents in some ways her parents' methods, often feeling that she lives in a deserted world, one which lacks the concreteness of traditional authority and encourages independent but subtly guided self-development. It is questionable, however, whether or not Anne would have resented far more the traditional authoritarian upbringing as expounded by Dussel. No doubt, under either system, the sensitive girl would have suffered the same "growing pains," but with the possibility of different results.

ISOLATION

Anne never writes of her being punished, although she complains bitterly of being criticized, reprimanded, and lectured. When she has behaved poorly, she might be ignored by the others for a day or so, but her parents do not practice such overt methods of punishment as the Van Daans, who send Peter off to his room without supper in one instance. The means by which Anne is disciplined are far more subtle. Moreover, as an exceedingly perceptive young person, she is able to sense the understated methods and to take on a large part of the burden of her own punishment and upbringing. This explains many of the lectures she gives herself in her diary. The entries of this nature are examples of her process of reasoning through her behavior and coming to terms with herself independent of overbearing external authority.

RESPONSIBILITY

The awareness of being responsible to and for her own actions is the basic cause for Anne's sense of isolation. Responsibility in itself is a lonely thing, for it eliminates the dependence on others with whom to share the blame or the praises which result from actions taken. That is why Anne so often writes to Kitty that she feels alone without the consolation of good advice or good examples. Having passed out of childhood, she realizes that she no longer qualifies for the amount of spoiling and protection children are permitted. Neither does she inherit the approval and acceptance of an adult. Confused by this status, she is apt to laugh or cry when neither reaction is desired, but either may occur from the emotional excess within her. She realizes that only through her own efforts will she successfully conquer her shortcomings.

LONELINESS

There are factors which contribute to Anne's sense of isolation other than the psychological phenomenon of adolescence itself and the loneliness of being responsible for her own actions, caused by her moderately progressive upbringing. There is to be considered the simple fact that among the inhabitants of the hideout there is no one particularly suitable with whom Anne can establish a natural friendship of the sort she enjoyed on the outside. People naturally tend to be selective in forming friendships, usually on the basis of similar interests, experiences, and age. Other than Peter, who is shy and at first does not appeal to Anne, there is no one in the group who fits the pattern Anne followed in making friends before going into hiding. Family relationships usually exist on a level different from that of friendship among peers (equals), although as children reach maturity, they are often apt to discover a solid friendship existing on an adult level with a brother, sister, or parent. But this does not usually occur until adulthood. Outside Anne's family group, the rest are strangers with whom she has a living arrangement and nothing more. True, she may discover areas of fondness for certain individuals among them, but the initial artificiality of their living in such close circumstances under conditions of duress does not provide a natural background for the formation of friendships. Thus, isolated from the real friends she has known prior to her existence in hiding, Anne must rely on her imagination either to summon up the memory of her former friends from school or to create the existence of a mythical friend such as Kitty, her diary. Anne is resourceful enough to do both of these things, but her loneliness grows even more from the natural fact that communication is a two-way process, and with imaginary friends, one lives in effect alone.

DEVELOPMENT OF STYLE

How has Anne's writing developed during the first year? It is likely that until now she has had neither the opportunity nor the necessity to write so extensively. With practice, one's skill is bound to improve, but since this is a privately practiced endeavor, there is no one to correct or comment on her writing. But there are other means by which Anne's skill may grow, and although less effective than correction by an authority, her writing is bound to improve. First of all, Anne reads a great deal. We may assume that the books are for the most part well-written by accomplished writers. They will necessarily have a subconscious effect on her own writing. It is relatively safe to assume that the few official flourishes which occur as noticeable breaks in her otherwise straightforward, unadorned style, are the results of her attempts to imitate the professional techniques of other writers. There are other passages in which one can detect by close examination the refinements in her own style. These occur in certain little ways such as the foreshortening of a descriptive passage into crisper, more pungent sentences lacking in the earlier amount of connectives. Another example is her developing sense of metaphor, by which suggestion and illusion replace long-windedness. And lastly, her sentence structure is becoming more complex, even though her tendency remains (perhaps as a permanent mark of personal style) to begin each paragraph with one short, simple, yet dramatic sentence.

MATURITY OF CONTENT

Her content is marked by a surprising objectivity, despite the personal nature of a work of this sort. It is as if she is able to step outside herself and see the character of Anne Frank at a distance, despite the obvious use of the first person pronoun. Her comments on the others in the group are also gaining in objectivity as she matures. Notice how she begins to rationalize their behavior rather than simply criticizing it. Notice, too, that her criticism usually has much validity and is not simply an outburst of cruel and petty complaints. On the other hand, we cannot fail to suspect Anne of selecting the most dramatic instances for illumination. This, however, bespeaks her selectivity of material as a potential writer.

THE DIARY OF A YOUNG GIRL

JULY 11, 1943–AUGUST 1, 1944: THE SECOND YEAR

THE ART OF LIVING

The first entry of the second year in hiding calls attention to the fact that Anne has matured in a particular aspect of the "Art of Living." She refers to her newly found practice of "shamming" in relations with other people instead of letting fly some plain talk as she had in the past. This is rather a sophisticated attitude on her part, reflecting one of the world's strange but true facts of human nature. What Anne has realized is that getting on well with others often requires deference to someone else's ego, and in the process, disregarding one's own. She has found that if she pretends to accept a situation or a remark rather than counter it with her own opinion, an argument will be avoided. Having arrived at this method of avoiding strife is still a somewhat new exercise in self-control, and Anne remarks that she often forgets her part in the little performance. Voicing opposition to an injustice without remembering what she has taught herself often has the earlier result. It is obvious that she is not especially content in this new knowledge, feeling that if she is in the right, she can be honest only by expressing herself rather than holding back. However, it seems likely that Anne, as others who mature, will discover that timing is the most important factor in presenting one's honest opinion. When this is learned, she will feel less like hypocrite and more adept at relationships when she can release her true feelings at the appropriate moment.

STOOPING TO CONQUER

The incident between Anne and Dussel over the use of the table in the room the two share is a good revelation of character as well as good example of Anne's competence as a writer. It has been mentioned previously that Dussel exemplifies the typical Old World attitude toward children. Assuming Anne's account to be fairly accurate, Mr. Dussel's behavior in this matter is less that of a tendency to bad manners than it is part of a pattern of thinking with regard to young people. Notice the way in which he minimizes Anne's need for the use of the table by making trifles of her work projects. To his way of thinking any child her age (Anne is now fourteen) could not possibly be engaged in serious work. Moreover, what probably tends to enrage Dussel all the more is Anne's mention of her rights. This notion is out of the question where Dussel is concerned, for "rights" have the connotation of dealings between equals. To Dussell, Anne is simply a child, and in no way does she have equal claim where privileges are concerned. Also noticeable are elements of Dussel's peevishness and Anne's capacity for getting around people. The incident is proof of the girl's new method of diplomacy. Rather than expounding on her rights and giving vent to her opinions on the subject, she allows Dussel to think he has won the match before she takes final action and with the help of her father gains the use of the table without causing a major clash within the group.

HUMOR AND JUSTICE

Regarding style, we notice the humorous overtones with which Anne has described an incident of combat in which she was personally involved without the aid of her sense of humor, the account could have become a petty, unpleasant attempt at self-justification and simply an outlet for her fury. Instead, the writer has drawn an incident between two characters with the objectivity of an observer. Read without the first person pronoun, the incident might easily pass for the work of an author using fictional characters for the purpose of illustrating the theme of justice. It should be evident to the reader by now, that justice is a subject with which Anne is both intellectually involved and personally concerned. Her illustrations of the topic are well noted for their pungence of tone as well as depth of exploration.

PRECOCIOUS CHILD'S THREAT

Often delightful to contemplate is the potential of a precocious child. It has already been cited that Anne was one of these exceptional children. Seen from another point of view, for instance from that of Mrs. Van Daan or Dussel, a youngster with Anne's perception and intelligence is far from a pleasure. To someone like Mrs. Van Daan, whose intelligence is rather average, a child such as Anne can pose a threat, for with added years and experience, the youngster will outstrip her elders and assume a position of superior importance. Allowing Mrs. Van Daan a fair share of vanity but not accusing her of being malicious, we may understand how it is to her advantage to keep Anne in her place, so to speak. Mr. Dussel, while not intellectually threatened by the girl, finds Anne a nuisance mainly because his life does not include much contact with children (he has none of his own) and because he finds fault with her upbringing. In the latter sense, he finds his position as an adult threatened by her. Allied in their respective weaknesses, Mr. Dussel and Mrs. Van Daan lose no opportunity to enhance their positions by finding fault with Anne. The procedure is not necessarily one which stems from cruelty, but more one arising from an instinct of self-protection. It is not an uncommon reaction of adults toward precocious children. In contrast, however, Mr. Frank's handling of his daughter is a much more positive one, although many parents feel equally threatened by exceptional children and react negatively in a manner similar to Mrs. Van Daan and Dussel.

A TYPICAL DAY

Anne gives a rather full account of a "typical day" in the hiding place. Notice that even here she is able to report the facts of their daily lives, but at the same time inject humor and a personal tone that is quite sophisticated for a fourteen-year old. Always observant of the little mannerisms each person displays, she makes the timetable seem alive with personalities rather than a mere tally sheet of dull routine. Considering the trying limitations of their activity, it seems astonishing that so much can be written about so pitifully little. But Anne, with the ability to observe more than surface action, creates an atmosphere of throbbing life filled to the brim with purposeful incident. Included in Anne's timetable is a critique of each character at the evening meal. This commentary resembles in many ways the anecdotes under photographs of students in a yearbook: witty, concise, and revealing. Notice here in this passage the mention of their protectors. Miep and Henk, Elli, Koophuis and Kraler function as more than sympathizers with a job to do. The helpers are almost members of the hideout, for they share the meals, conversation, and above all, the danger involved in protecting Jews against Nazi regulations. Having thus sealed their fate with the inhabitants, they are considered full-fledged members of the little community. Despite the strain on personalities, each person, occupant or protector, has achieved a vital function in the underground corporation.

FEAR AND STILLNESS

Anne mentions over and over the two things that disturb her the most-the fear and the stillness. These are the enemies with which she cannot cope as successfully as she can with interpersonal problems. The "stillness" to which Anne refers is especially oppressive on Sundays. This is mainly because there is no business activity downtown where they live and because of the war, very few people spend the day enjoying strolls along the streets. If anyone is to be seen through the slit in the curtains, it is usually someone in a great hurry to reach a destination. Grim faced and war weary, the once bustling populace now keeps to its shelters. With nothing to do and no people to hear or watch engaged in the weekday routine, Anne finds the stillness quite terrifying, almost like that of a deserted world. This atmosphere gives rise to thoughts that the usual amount of activity can keep away. It promotes reflection and brings to mind those horrors of war which Anne must continually fight in order to avoid depression and despair. Reading and sleep are the only methods of combatting the oppressive stillness and the fear it brings. She feels at these times even more alienated from those with whom she shares the life in hiding.

NEW IDEAS

Once again, Mr. Frank comes to the aid of his daughters whose intellectual appetites are never satisfied. For Margot, he has arranged a correspondence course in Latin which she will take in Elli's name. For Anne, however, he has selected the New Testament-a subject that necessarily seems incompatible with the Franks' religious beliefs. It appears that Margot finds the idea of a New Testament rather strange and feels uncomfortable about the thought of such a book as a Chanukah gift for Anne. Mr. Frank agrees and it is decided that the gift will be for St. Nicholas Day. Consider for a moment the motives behind a Jewish father giving his daughter the New Testament. It appears that Mr. Frank is a broad-minded man whose intellect far exceeds his personal prejudices. Is it not compatible, too, with the modern methods by which he is raising his daughters for Mr. Frank to want Anne to be exposed to the fundamental ideas on which her civilization is base? Perhaps, too, he feels that the philosophy of Jesus may lift Anne's spirits, and that the content of the New Testament will help her to understand her own religion better. By opening up such a broad area of thought to his daughter, Mr. Frank may have provided Anne with endless hours of intellectual occupation. Comparing the selection of new studies for Anne and Margot, one can detect the subtle differences in each girl's mental preferences and capabilities. Anne considers Margot her intellectual superior, but notice how the older girl tends to prefer the narrower, more disciplined aspects of study, while the younger girl seeks the broader, more interpretive ones. Both girls are obviously quite intelligent, and Anne's feeling of inferiority to Margot is probably more the result of their differences in age and personality.

IMAGINATION

The quality of Anne's imagination is evident in all her entries, but particularly so when she tries to relate her past, present, and future existence to a larger system of being which will unify the three. She finds it difficult to conceive that she, Anne, in her present life of hiding, was ever the other girl who lived among other people, went to school, had friends, enjoyed sports, and had a big roomy house occupied by only one family. That seems to be a different, dimly recalled person, a shadowy figure who is as remote as the Anne who will emerge after the war. The possibility of resuming the old life is less of a reality than she would like to believe because the oppressive atmosphere of the present is too forcefully at work on her senses. Thus, she finds that her every mood and thought is affected by the immediacies of every day, and she wishes to free her spirit of this dependence. A noble thought, but almost impossible. Contemplating a mode of life after the war is far more difficult because so much of the life she has known is distorted by the past and the present. She knows that much physical destruction has taken place, and that the facilities of life will be greatly changed. But the precocious girl is equally aware of the spiritual and psychological changes that have occurred in the people, both those with whom she lives and those on the outside. More brutal than these intuitions is the knowledge that many of the people she has known are dead. From these thoughts, Anne's imagination develops a beautiful metaphor of her isolation which approaches allegory in its attempt to make concrete all that she finds so unreal.

GHASTLY PROPHECY

In describing the accident which befell her fountain pen, Anne endows her lost possession with a personality of its own. This is not a peculiar idea, for many inanimate objects have been personified in the imaginations of their owners. The fate of the fountain pen gives rise to a chilling prophecy which Anne makes unintentionally. The pen has been cremated, and that is the fate Anne wishes for herself after death, not realizing the ghastly nearness of it all.

DREAMS AND GUILT

Weighing even more heavily on Anne's mind is her former school friend, Lies Goosens. The entry in the diary concerning Anne's vision of her friend is heartrending-almost prayerful. How desperately Anne reaches out for Lies, through the mists of memory leading into remorse. One wonders just what insignificant act of girlish jealousy occurred that causes Anne to feel so guilty. More likely it is guilt of another kind that brings to Anne's memory the minor incident of rivalry over a new friendship Lies had made. The guilt Anne really feels is quite understandable. She and her family are safe from the Nazis and rather comfortable in the little world they have created for themselves. In spite of the difficulties they incur in the confinement of their everyday life, there is no comparison to the horrors and privations which have befallen Lies and her family. It is as if Anne wishes to repent for her own well-being, and Lies is an identifiable symbol through whom Anne can reach the unknown thousands of persecuted people in sympathy and regret. The haunting image of Lies is indicative of Anne's imagination in still another capacity-one far from the humorous side that shows most often-that other "deeper, finer" side which Anne feels too shy to reveal to anyone but Kitty thus far.

FEMININE MODESTY

When Anne is ill with the flu, many home remedies are applied and Dussel, who has had medical training feels it is his responsibility to give the sick girl professional attention. Notice Anne's revulsion toward his physical presence in such close contact to her own body. This is indicative of more than just the shyness of a young girl whose sense of her physical maturity is confusing. Anne's attitude reveals an awareness of developing sensuality, the earliest longings of womanhood. She is resentful of physical contact with Dussel because he is not the appropriate image of her young fancy. Rather, she has too many other associations with Dussel, and the nearness of the older man embarrasses and upsets her because of their established relationship. Like so many girls undergoing similar phases of development, Anne rejects the very longing itself because it is unfamiliar, and when stimulated by unsuitable and unexpected incidents, her reaction is naturally one of disgust and rejection. Before or after this awkward phase, Dussel's medical attention would pass unnoticed in any way out of the ordinary. Considering Dussel's attitude toward Anne, it is even less likely that there is anything improper about his examining or treating her. Later Anne reads a book which explains this awkward and exaggerated physical modesty.

CONFINEMENT

How painful it must be for Anne to hear of Koophuis' daughter, Corry, and her active life in the outside world. Yet Anne must again remind herself that if Corry is fortunate in comparison to her, she is that much more fortunate in comparison to other Jewish children not safely hidden away from the persecutors. Anne's longing for fun and freedom is another of the great tortures she is teaching herself to endure. Her methods are difficult, for no amount of rationalizing can compensate for the absence of someone or something unattainable. The strength and courage shown by Anne in fighting these seizures of longing are admirable. Reluctantly she admits that when strong substitutional thinking fails, her only relief is tears. One wonders about the effects of such frustrations on the young, and marvels further at the absence of bitterness or cynicism in Anne's overall thinking.

NEW FAMILY ATTITUDES

Reading through the pages of Anne's diary we notice the changes of her attitude toward her father. Now, just past midway, it becomes evident that there is a development in her feelings about Pim (Mr. Frank) which indicates her maturity, her own process of development from a little girl into a woman. Mr. Frank was right a year and a half before in saying that Anne would outgrow her "Oedipal" crush on her father. No longer one of childish hero worship, nor the uncomfortable possessiveness toward an imaginary lover, Anne's concept of her father has become mature in that he exists as an equal insofar as his human suffering and experiences are concerned. Of course, he is still held in the exalted position of "Daddy," but this is now tempered by Anne's own experiences of pain and longing,. of trial and triumph. Now he can confide in his younger daughter those things with which he would trust an adult. Out of their former closeness has grown a special sort of friendship not uncommon among members of a family who are similar in nature and spirit. Anne has worked very hard to gain this friendship and confidence, often overextending herself, and at times withdrawing. Mr. Frank has stood by watching his daughter mature, always holding his feeling for her within the bounds of discretion so that his wife and other daughter had their fair share of his affections. Now, if there is favoritism, it is not of the destructive kind which can occur in families, but the natural preference of kindred souls meeting on a spiritual and intellectual level of communication. Anne feels with well-grounded confidence that those special interchanges of thought between her and her father do not extend to the other members of the family despite his genuine affection for all of them.

SUFFERING

What should also be evident is that Anne's concept of suffering has broadened beyond the self-centered sort in which she at first indulged to the exclusion of others' pain. True, she felt remotely the sense of suffering experienced by those in the outside world-especially those she had known. But what has occurred is a deepening sense of humanity, the ability to both sympathize and identify with the pain of others. This comes only from a variety of painful experiences coupled with the ability to see beyond the pain as a self-contained experience, and to cultivate an objectivity in suffering which relates the individual experience to that of others in ever widening circles until all humanity is encompassed. This is a concept that does not necessarily come equally to those who mature chronologically. Many adults do not identify with the pain of others to a great extent, although they may give limited recognition to others' suffering. Mrs. Van Daan, for example, is an adult who reacts to pain in this limited way, not feeling terribly far outside herself that which others have undergone. In contrast, Mr. Frank is the sort of individual whose experiences of pain, although kept to himself for the most part, extend beyond his own immediate feelings, and generate a sympathy for humankind. Anne is in the process of developing this quality of depth, one which is as intense as poetry and as deep as philosophy. Notice how she is moved in her writing to both poetic and philosophical expression. Notice, too, her understanding of painful experience as the source of her father's tolerance, and her hope that she, too, may learn from his example.

NEW YEAR'S REFLECTIONS

Looking back on the entries in her diary, Anne notes the outbursts of fury against her mother which, at this point, seem quite shocking and cause her pangs of conscience. Wishing to clarify the record, and to indicate her present understanding of why those entries were so unattractively one-sided, Anne reflects on her behavior and attitude. She first discusses the reasons for having written so tempestuously, realizing that many of these outbursts were the outlets for moods now dealt with differently. Wisely, she recognizes the ways in which she has matured, so that she no longer has such a one-sided view of people, and her mother in particular. In a calm and adult manner, Anne accepts the facts that 1) she and her mother do not basically understand each other, and may never do so, even though they can get along by exercising patience and restraint, and, 2) that her love for her mother is not of the customary dependent sort experienced in similar relationships. It takes great effort on the part of a child to come to terms with these uncomfortable notions. It is easier to write off one or the other party as altogether wrong and to go through life with that idea firmly fixed. But because Anne wishes more than anything to understand fully the secrets and peculiarities of human nature, she is willing to continue her efforts of exploration into both sides of every question-even the most painful ones about the closest relationships. Her search for the reason behind the conflicts with her mother culminates temporarily in her realization that Mrs. Frank desires to be "friends" with her daughters rather than a typical parent. This explains the gaping need Anne has felt for maternal authority which would have set an example. Anne has had to find in her imagination her image of what a mother should be. But one must not be too hasty to condemn Mrs. Frank's attitude as it is very common for children to feel alienated by one or both parents and to create an idealized parental figure for compensation. Much of what Anne feels is valid and understandable, but the problem works both ways. No doubt Mrs. Frank feels equally alienated by a precocious daughter who favors her father. For a person as sensitive as Anne, the experience of growing up is so much more difficult that Mrs. Frank has stepped aside, for better or for worse, realizing that she cannot cope with the situation though she might well long to do so. In time, it seems inevitable for Anne to understand and accept more about her mother as an individual and fret less about the ideal parent she imagines should exist.

DREAMS OF THE PAST

From out of Anne's short past comes the image of Peter Wessel in a dream so real that Anne has the sensation of his touch upon her cheek. Recalling that of all her "boy friends" from former days, Peter Wessel was the one she secretly cared for, the reader should have no trouble understanding how Anne's present state of loneliness could cause her to invoke his memory so powerfully and with such a strong sense of desire. In a similarly vivid way, Anne has dreamt of Lies and both grandmothers. Such dreams indicate the sense of closeness Anne has felt for these people, but has never been able to communicate fully. Therefore, in dreams, she goes back to individuals from her past, fulfilling in this capacity the incomplete relationships. Naturally, these dreams are motivated by her extreme loneliness and intense desire to be close to someone. Notice how the release of these emotions by the dream process affects Anne and how much better she feels physically and mentally.

A LOVE OBJECT

Another important aspect of Anne's dream of Peter Wessel is her developing sexual maturity. Convinced that she has always understood "the longing," at least in her mind, Anne is now beginning to experience it physically. Having discussed such matters with her parents, more so with her father, Anne has also read a book for young girls on the topic. Although she understands much in theory, the reality of physical desire developing within her body fascinates and delights her. Again we see how Anne is able to take an objective view of personal experience, and thus be an observer of her inmost self. The result of this added process of maturity causes in Anne an even more desperate need for a love object. Because of this need, her fantasy of Peter Wessel becomes more understandable. Note, however, Anne's sense of propriety and restraint where matters of physical affection are concerned. She may feel her love for the boy of her past to be complete, but she will not be permissive, even in fantasy. He may touch only her face. For Anne, the dream of Peter Wessel signals an entirely new phase in her life. It changes her attitudes to relationships with others and also affects her feelings about herself. The need for a love object has been satisfied at least in fantasy by Peter Wessel. A sense of fulfillment has given Anne a different perspective now that she has found an object for her emotions. Yet, we know that imaginary companionship is not totally satisfying. What develops emotionally for Anne henceforth will be more understandable in terms of this notion.

LOVE TRANSFER

Just after Anne's dream of Peter Wessel, she finds herself suddenly interested in getting to know Peter Van Daan whom she has virtually ignored for the past year and a half. While she seems to be surprised at her newly found interest in him, the reader should consider it a natural outgrowth of the dream. In more specialized terminology, Anne's interest and eventual romantic friendship with Peter Van Daan would be called a "transference." This means simply that love is transferred from one object to another, seeking with each change the satisfaction unattainable with the previous one. With Anne, the pattern is quite basic and not all unnatural. The primary image, of course, is an ideal figure. At the very first it is her father. Maturing both intellectually and emotionally, she realizes that her father is not "the one." The second ideal figure is Peter Wessel. But again, the transfer has been from one unattainable object to another. The next object is Peter Van Daan. He is real and attainable, and Anne transfers the ideal image to him along with her affections. It will be interesting to see how she discovers that the ideal of love must be tempered by the faults and imperfections of the love object.

ANNE AND PETER

At first, Anne suffers the pangs of uncertainty which every new relationship between members of the opposite sex entails. The flirtation, withdrawal, anxiety, and infatuation fill the moments of Anne's newly discovered world Little by little she becomes less afraid of being a nuisance to Peter, and he in turn, gradually overcomes his shyness. Intelligently, Anne senses behind his awkwardness and former habit of solitude a longing as deep as hers for companionship, the need for comfort and understanding. Skillfully she draws him out of his shell, at the same time delighting in the new meaning he has given her life. He has provided her with the security she craved, and now this confidence of his affection for her enables her to be less defensive with the other occupants. Her relationships with all of them are markedly improved, most noticeably with her mother, sister, and Mrs. Van Daan. This is because she has found her identity as a woman in the relationship with Peter. Maintaining discretion and restraint in their physical affection is important to both young people, and Mr. Franks heart-to-heart talk with each one separately helps them to understand how vitally important self-control is in their confining circumstances. Nevertheless, the mild aspects of physical love are for both Anne and Peter important as marks of their maturity. In Anne's commentary, one can detect her objective interest in the subject itself, again displaying an unusually mature and perceptive attitude. While the grownups are pleased that Anne and Peter have found each other, they take a dim view of the possible consequences of too strong an attachment. Despite the teasing and occasionally somewhat stern remarks made by the adults, the two young people manage quite well to conduct their relationship on a satisfying and wholesome level.

REALISM

Aside from Anne's relationship with Peter Van Daan, the second most important aspect of her maturity this second year is her developing sense of realism. Because she is basically an idealist,

Anne has suffered more from the painful realities of life than those with a less lofty notion of the perfect way the world and its inhabitants should be. This is not to say that Anne has lost her ideals-far from it. But what has occurred is a tempering of them with experiences and deep thinking which have combined to teach her that although one has the right to expect much, one must be grateful for even a fraction's realization of what was expected. In connection with this, Anne has learned to expect as much from herself as from others. A problem growing out of the sense of self-reliance is just a little overdose of independence which disturbs her parents, and particularly her father whom she hurts deeply at one point but is then forgiven. Anne derives a new source of strength and conviction from her realistic attitude. For one so young, it may seem to the reader rather frightening that Anne now sees each moment of life in the here and now to hold more importance than the vague, distant future. It may seem an almost cynical attitude, until consideration is given to the effects of the war and primarily to the immediacy of death that has been, perhaps, the most forceful influence in shaping Anne's seemingly hard realism. This is basically a form of protection against pain, the kind of intense suffering with which Anne has had to deal at the risk of losing her sanity. Grief cannot be tolerated by most people in overly large quantities, and very sensitive individuals are most prone to emotional disorders when they cannot cope with mental and spiritual anguish. Miraculously, through deliberate and tireless effort, Anne has learned to cope with her suffering and to find ways of relief by thinking things through to a suitable conclusion. Accepting the brutalities of the present was probably for her the most difficult task, for her imagination was enabled to escape by projecting back into the past or forward into the future. However as the past became more remote and the future more uncertain, Anne had to accept the present, and then it was all meaningful. In strengthening her sense of reality, she has also done much to reinforce her ideals by making them conform to a more practical pattern. That is, she has learned to accept the possibility that every person and situation may fall short of perfection, but that she can still seek it in striving to improve herself and give aid to others who also seek perfectability. One does not usually come to this wisdom at such an early age, and it is a remarkable achievement to watch its development as we read Anne's diary.

SELF-OBSERVER

Often reflecting on the girl she used to be, Anne has cataloged her own development with wisdom, emotion, objectivity, and honesty. She has experienced all the phases of maturity to date as both participant and observer. Her accomplishments are commendable, for she has undertaken the responsibility of growing up as her own obligation. She has developed a concept of life that strives for idealism, but does not deny the imperfections of humanity. Although she still has her moments of doubt and rejection, of fear and uncertainty, Anne's over-all outlook is one of positivism toward life. It is manifested as the diary progresses by improvements in her relationships with others. If she cannot accept them totally, she can at least understand why not, and can find a rapport with each one based on the qualities which she finds acceptable. She endeavors to see the best in people, and to bring out the best in herself even when it would be easier to give in to selfishness and self-interest. Anne is able to care for those people in whom she finds weakness, and to be truthful about her emotions. For example, she knows that she is not seriously in love with Peter Van Daan, but finds value in the affection they feel for each other. She realizes that he is more dependent on her than she on him, but feels she can help him as he has helped her. She is disappointed about his weaknesses, but does not close her mind to the possibility that he might improve.

Anne has also come to terms with her parents and her sister, appreciating them for what they are, not despising them for not being what she selfishly wishes them to be. She has cultivated a realistic sense of the future and the possibility that it might not exist. She has acquired goals which are valuable for the present even if they can never be realized.

LASTING PHILOSOPHY

The events move along swiftly toward the end of the second year. The Allied invasion of Normandy has occurred, and all anticipate the liberation of Holland. Now Anne's political commentary is more opinionated and occurs more frequently. The end of their confinement seems near. The war tells on the inhabitants. Mrs. Van Daan is very near a severe case of hysteria. All are impatient, frightened, hopeful. Anne has been accepted as an equal by the younger generation of the hideout who have formed a faction with rather definite ideas that differ from those of the grownups. The young people have found a sense of group identity and no longer function as selfish and competitive individuals to the degree that they did previously. Anne has gone up in their estimation, and she is rather surprised at their complimentary comments. While there are still quarrels among them all, they do not seem to disturb Anne as severely. The strain tells on their protectors.

The last few entries summarize Anne's philosophy of life. She is aware of her development, aware that she has matured, perhaps beyond her years. Still introspective, she is capable of self-reproach and depression. But her over-all attitude is one of positivism-a belief so forceful that she is certain it can sustain her no matter what happens. It is curious that the last entry is so wistful, so melancholy with self-inquiry. One turns the page expecting a new note of optimism the next day. But there is nothing more. The end of the book comes as unexpectedly as the end of safety in hiding came to the eight occupants. Yet it is not the end, for in the world's memory, Anne Frank lives on, an example of faith, courage, and spirit. Her diary is an enduring testimonial to the power of positivism itself to prevail over despair.

THE DIARY OF A YOUNG GIRL

CHARACTER ANALYSES

It has been said that the characters in *The Diary of A Young Girl* are one-dimensional because they are presented from only one point of view. While this idea is not technically untrue, it is too easy a way of avoiding the reader's responsibility to investigate the other angles of vision made possible in many subtle ways. Aside from what Anne tells us directly about the other seven members of the group, their actions in various situations as well as their remarks permit us to make inferences of our own regarding their basic character. Another aspect in the reader's favor is the limited background in which the characters carry out their actions. With a broader range of setting and background in which to disguise many facets of their personalities, the eight major characters might never reveal their basic personality traits as they are forced to do within the confines of their hiding place. In such a case, we would necessarily be forced to accept without question the author's point of view. However, the limited setting aids the reader to determine for himself the validity of the author's description and to make his own decisions regarding aspects of personality which the author's youth and mood might have caused her to overlook. It will be interesting to contrast the author's description of character with the reader's perception and to determine the comparative validity of each.

MAJOR CHARACTERS

Anne

Introduced by herself as a thirteen-year-old German-Jewish girl living in Holland with her parents and sister to avoid Nazi persecution, she states the purpose of her diary as one of unburdening her innermost thoughts in letters to an imaginary friend. The reason she needs this sort of companion is because in real life no one exists in whom she can confide utterly. Early in her diary, Anne reveals her flaws of chattering in a "know-all" fashion, resenting her mother and sisters, and generally upsetting the others by her immature behavior. She also displays a rebellious attitude toward criticism and correction from adults, especially since she does not see in them the perfected human beings she would like as examples to follow. Her resentment of her mother in the early stages of the diary is mostly the result of an Oedipal rivalry with the woman for the love of the father on whom Anne childishly dotes. Her attitude toward Margot is also the result of a sibling rivalry in which children quite naturally compete for their parents' love. Anne has less desire to emulate her older sister's qualities of intelligence, good behavior, and good looks, but instead wishes to be loved as an individual on her own merits. Anne feels that her sister ignores her and that her mother is not competent to understand her. Hence, she withdraws from them and seeks solace in her father's affection and approval.

Having been cut off from the natural outlets of friends, school, sports, and other entertainment, Anne is forced inward upon herself and finds her chief occupation in the early months of hiding one of self-criticism, analysis, and justification. She is an emotionally and intellectually sensitive girl whose tendency is to be precocious in that her understanding exceeds her experience in many ways. Forced into an unnatural and uncomfortable situation by the emergency living arrangement, Anne finds it extraordinarily difficult to achieve the self-control necessary in order to get along with the others and at the same time maintain her independence as an individual. Her desire for approval and acceptance conflicts with her equal need to excel and be recognized. Her theories do not always find compatibility with her actions because of the added emotional strain of such confined living.

As strongly as she criticizes the others, she is equally as harsh with herself. She is a perfectionist and an idealist whose sensitivity often causes her to feel rejected and alone in her "valiant" attempt to be "good." By the same token, she rejects the others on the grounds of their imperfections. But more important is the fact that because she is in the stage of maturity known as adolescence, she cannot always account either to herself or others for her extremes of mood and seemingly inconsistent behavior. Hence, she withdraws deep into herself, feeling that if anyone can understand it is she alone. Months of trying with mixed results of success and failure bring Anne to a greater understanding of her former self and present self. She is aware of her previous childishness and her present maturity, but she has not found her introverted life very satisfying. Her major discovery after the first year is that she is lonely-incredibly and passionately lonely.

Having outgrown some of her selfish and self-centered patterns of behavior, she is ready to try relating to the others in her newly discovered way. This is a method whereby she will restrain herself at all costs even when she knows she is pretending to an attitude of concession and feeling just the opposite inside. To her surprise and wry pleasure, the new method works so far as her limited self-control extends. She has ceased to resent her mother for the old reasons, has learned to love her father in a different, less dependent way, and has begun to perceive her sister as a less remote creature who might possibly be a girl with needs and feelings basically similar to her own although manifested differently by virtue of personal individuality.

Having suffered intensely the worst aspects of "growing pains," Anne feels an almost smug sense of her own independence and self-reliance. Realizing that her sudden growing up was probably precipitated by the change in living and the effects of the war, she resents the concentrated anguish it caused her, but appreciates her new maturity for the power it now gives her. This power is rooted in self-knowledge from which develops a new and more sympathetic attitude toward the others. Able to expect more from herself, she demands less from those about her. She understands their failings now because she has come to terms with her own. Her approach to life is conducted on a more realistic basis. Yet she has remained firm in her ideals realizing that only strong faith, courage, and hope will see her through these dark moments which she knows must be experienced by oneself alone. A sense of guilt hovers over her reflections of past behavior, but she is determined to re-establish her relationships on a more mature level.

With all her introspective activity and the satisfaction gained by her inner struggle, she is still disturbed by an unremitting loneliness and the need to give and receive affection. As the relationship she seeks cannot be conducted with a member of her family nor with one of the other adults, she transfers her idealized image of Peter Wessel from her memory to the person of Peter Van Daan. Because of her growing emotional and physical maturity, it necessarily follows a pattern of affection which is more than a friendship but less than love, yet a relationship which satisfies both needs. Having found a love object, Anne is now secure enough to drop many of her leftover defenses. This is manifested in her latest attitude toward others which shows more humility and compassion, coupled with more courage and tact in asserting her independence as a young adult. Yet Anne is not without her problems. She is still moody and frequently disappointed in herself and others. Much of this dissatisfaction, however, comes more from without than from within, for the effects of war and life in hiding have told on Anne as well as the others.

SUMMARY

On the positive side, Anne is exceptionally intelligent, courageous, honest, forthright, able to understand others and herself, eager for perfection, and willing to work hard. Negatively she is difficult and temperamental at times, can be tactless and occasionally quite stubborn.

Margot

In contrast to Anne, Margot is less outspoken, more mature, and more reserved. In comparison, she is intelligent but more disciplined and directed into narrower fields of scholarly interest. Aware of her younger sister's sensitivity and often hostile attitude, Margot ignores Anne rather than increase the rivalry by active participation. Occasionally, she will defend herself with a caustic or catty remark, but for the most part shies away from combat. More inclined to be like her mother, Margot

seeks the companionship of Mrs. Frank in preference to that
of her father. Because she is older and closer to womanhood,
she is better able to understand her mother's problems. In
addition, Margot and her mother seem to have similar reactions
to various situations, a fact that would necessarily explain
their compatibility. Margot, too, suffers from loneliness and
fear caused by the war, but hers is more of a quiet desperation
manifested in poor sleep and appetite, extreme fatigue and
self-containment. As Anne matures, Margot extends the hand
of sisterly friendship, sensing Anne's need for a confidante and
companion. She is much less timid in her approach to Anne
than vice-versa. Margot understands Anne far better than the
younger girl probably realizes, yet does not force herself upon
her sister when Anne withdraws. Margot is exceedingly gracious
and wise in her reaction to Anne's and Peter's relationship.
Margot complains little and endures much. In this way, she is a
great deal like her father.

SUMMARY

Positively, Margot is tactful, reserved, mature, intelligent,
industrious, understanding, and for the most part
considerate of others. Negatively, she is capable of being
catty, is almost too self-contained, and often sides with her
mother against Anne rather than abstaining from quarrels
as seems to be her more usual custom.

Mrs. Frank

A woman from a background of wealth and culture, Mrs. Frank
is attractive, literate, and accustomed to a comfortable life. She
has a rather progressive outlook on parenthood, considering her
daughters more as friends than subordinate offspring. As the

object of rivalry with her younger daughter for the love of Mr. Frank, the woman attempts to reach Anne through the only kind of love she can offer, but finding herself rejected, turns for solace and companionship to her older daughter Margot. Trusting her husband to see Anne through this Oedipal phase, Mrs. Frank cannot resist continued attempts to secure Anne's love, and failing to do so, often retaliates for the rejection by reprimanding the young girl for faulty behavior. A fairly intense woman whose background has not prepared her for the hardships inflicted by the war, Mrs. Frank suffers initially from shock and fear in the new quarters. Once a pattern of living has been established, she complies as far as possible with what is expected of her, often leaning, however, on Mrs. Van Daan to perform the more menial tasks for which Mrs. Frank is ill-trained. Rarely complaining but showing the effects of war in much the same ways as Margot, Mrs. Frank bears the burden of the war with forced calm and controlled silence. The relationship between Mr. and Mrs. Frank is marred very seldom by disagreements or outbursts of any sort. Those which do arise are usually the result of Anne's offensiveness toward her mother to which the older woman reacts with tears and an appeal to her husband for help. Her role is that of dependence on her husband who protects her with wisdom and affection, often shielding her from anything which might be upsetting. Mrs. Frank's strength of character is of a dependent rather than independent nature, and she can be relied upon for endurance and sympathy, trust and compassion so long as she herself feels protected.

SUMMARY

Positively Mrs. Frank is courageous and carefully controlled; she is gracious, well-bred and intelligent. Her strength comes from a source of dependence on her husband in whose love she feels protected and can thereby give sympathy and encouragement to others if called upon to do so. Negatively, Mrs. Frank is ill-prepared for the discomforts of war, leaning heavily on the others to function in areas where she is weak. Often unable to cope with her precocious younger daughter, she occasionally resorts either to forcing love or heaping reprimands on Anne.

Mr. Frank

A man of courage and foresight, Mr. Frank has planned far in advance how he will protect his family from the perils of Nazi persecution. He has been the organizer and chief instrument of an elaborate underground arrangement whereby he can remain in Holland, keep his family safe, and still guide his business indirectly. Born into wealth and culture, Mr. Frank has sufficiently become a man of the world to utilize his powers of courage and intelligence against the most unfavorable odds. His intellect and sensitivity are great sources of strength which he shares with others. He is judicious and wise, looked upon by the others as leader, peacemaker, and confidant. He never openly reveals his troubles, but contains them as well as the problems of others. His suffering is made evident only by certain facial expressions or detachments into his intellectual pursuits. His relationships are strained only by others' intense dependence on him. He is able to cope with family difficulties by distributing his loyalty and affection equally among his wife and two daughters although it seems that Anne requires just a little extra attention and care.

SUMMARY

Positively, Mr. Frank is a man of courage, strength and ideals. He is skilled in intellectual and practical matters. His capabilities enable others to look upon him as a leader, peacemaker, and confidant. He is judicious in his relations with others, applying wisdom and tolerance in difficult situations. He is able to distribute his attention equally among the members of his own family. He does not reveal his problems to anyone, often retaining tension to his own detriment. Negatively, Mr. Frank is perhaps a bit too self-contained and perhaps able to dominate the others by means of his exalted position which no one dares to refute. Occasionally, he seems to take Anne's part where she might have learned more from handling a situation alone.

Peter Van Daan

Throughout most of the period in hiding Peter is shy, awkward, and intent upon keeping to himself. His relationship with his parents seems to be relatively free from strife except for occasional instances in which he needs to be disciplined. These do not seem to be indicative of extraordinary misbehavior on his part nor undue harshness on his parents' side. Peter displays manliness and courage in attending to the patrol and inspection duties assigned to him. His affection is mainly expressed by his love for his cat Mouschi and the office cat, Boche. His attempts to express affection for the others seems to be limited by his late adolescent awkwardness. He is reasonably intelligent but has neither the drive nor the discipline for studies displayed by Anne and Margot. As an outlet for the pressures of confined living, he sleeps a great deal, stays alone, and often lets off steam in solitary outbursts of profanity in the attic. He appears to be cordial and well-mannered. When annoyed he either retreats or becomes tongue-tied in an attempt to express his anger. He resents having been born a Jew and thus victimized by Hitler's anti-Semitic legislation. His ambitions for adulthood are uncertain and he professes a desire to be a gambler or loafer after the war.

He is often quite cynical. In many ways, he is less intellectually curious than Anne and his interests are more mundane. He scoffs at her ideals and displays a superficial attitude toward life that she finds disconcerting. Much of this may be bluster and an act to make him appear aloof and more masculine, but some of it is genuinely indicative of a characteristic weakness and the desire to make life easy. His emotional dependence on Anne eventually exceeds hers on him, but this is most likely the effects of first love on a young man who has never opened himself to anyone before. Peter is gentle and discreet with Anne, never taking physical or emotional advantage of their affectionate relationship.

SUMMARY

Positively, Peter is gentle, well-mannered alert, intelligent, courageous, and willing to do his share of the work. Negatively, he is shy and withdrawn, often cynical, not overly ambitious for his future, and concerned with very mundane matters.

Mrs. Van Daan

A woman of different background from that of Anne's mother, Mrs. Van Daan tends to be more open in her emotions, often to the distress of others. She is flirtatious, vain, and often petty. She tends to be more hysterical in her reactions to the effects of the war, often suffering acutely from strange delusions of harm and death. On the other hand, she has a warmth and generosity that is easily displayed if properly encouraged. Mrs. Van Daan is much more domestically capable than Mrs. Frank and undertakes more than her share of the household duties. Her intelligence is rather limited and she often says things which display her lack of wisdom and cause mirth for the others. She tends also to be more old-fashioned in her outlook on childrearing that the progressive Franks, and enjoys expressing uncalled for opinions on this and other topics, often causing more disagreement among the others than is necessary. She is somewhat jealous of Anne because of the girl's superior intelligence and her ability to draw Peter into her confidence. However, she is often the one Anne can discuss things with openly if the topic is not too controversial.

SUMMARY

Positively, Mrs. Van Daan is capable of warmth and understanding. She is also a good housewife and attends to more than her share of the domestic duties. Negatively, she is vain, possessive, and often quarrelsome. She can be unnecessarily coquettish and petty. The war has caused her to border on hysteria.

Mr. Van Daan

Seemingly a competent man, Mr. Van Daan is noted for his general reliability and willingness to undertake his share of responsibility. He tends, however, to be obdurate, and considers his opinions irrefutable. He is a stern but loving father to Peter. His relationship with his wife is highlighted but not necessarily marred by coarse, loud bickering which both seem to thrive upon. He does not display a particularly keen intellect, but he is well-informed in general matters and prefers talk of politics in which he can exercise his opinions. He seems to be rather firmly constituted and is able to withstand many pressures but becomes particularly unnerved by short cigarette rations and complains readily when he does not feel well.

SUMMARY

Positively, Mr. Van Daan is reliable, willing to work, and reasonably courageous. Negatively, he is very opinionated and given to coarse, frequent arguments with his wife.

Mr. Dussel

An older man, childless, and lonesome for his wife, Mr. Dussel seems more often than not to exhibit a peevishness and desire to be let alone typical of fussy bachelors. He is often inconsiderate in his habits. On the other hand, he has the facility to remove himself from the quarrels of the others as he finds their outbursts detestable and unnerving. He is critical, particularly of the young for whom he has limited patience. He is somewhat of an "Old World gentleman," retaining certain formalities which add a touch of grandeur not only to his personality but to the lives of the others. He seeks for the most part to be uninvolved, finding solitude and comfort in his mysterious work projects which take up most of his waking hours. He is not terribly sympathetic to others' problems, finding it easier to ignore them than become involved at the expense of forfeiting his aloofness. When he does become involved in squabbles, his intense discomfort in such situations causes him to act pedantic, and almost childishly unreasonable. He is also capable of graciousness and a limited amount of compassion, although it is apparent that in his lonesomeness he is becoming somewhat bitter and a rather sad figure.

SUMMARY

Positively, Dussel is quiet, self-contained, industrious and usually polite. Negatively, he is peevish, somewhat inconsiderate in his personal habits, and unreasonably stubborn when infrequently involved in squabbles. His loneliness has caused him to be considerably withdrawn, solitary, and possibly somewhat bitter.

MINOR CHARACTERS

Miep And Henk Van Santen

A devoted couple in the employ of Mr. Frank, they are solid, reliable, and loyal to their Jewish friends. Their willingness to work tirelessly and to take incredible risks indicates the high caliber of their characters. They are typical of those engaged in the activities of the Dutch underground whose unselfish acts of loyalty and courage earned the entire world's admiration.

Elli Vossen

A girl in her early twenties employed as a secretary in Mr. Frank's business, Elli is another courageous, loyal member of the Dutch underground. She, too, is unselfishly devoted to those in hiding, working hard and spending her nerves in faithful service spread too thin among her responsibilities to her job, father, fiance, and eight Jewish friends.

Kraler And Koophuis

Friends and business associates of long-standing, these men are the mainstays of Mr. Frank's commercial and personal interests. Bearing more than their share of responsibility takes its toll on Kraler's nerves and Koophuis physical condition, but they are tirelessly loyal and hardworking to the very end. For their activities in the Dutch underground, both were sentenced by the Nazis to serve terms in Dutch concentration camps. Both men returned alive after the liberation of Holland to bear testimony against the Nazis.

THE DIARY OF A YOUNG GIRL

CRITICAL COMMENTARY

Because this is the single work of a young author, only a very limited amount of critical material is available on *The Diary of a Young Girl*. There are other factors, too, which have bearing on the scarcity of written commentary about Anne Frank's work. A diary in form, and non-fiction in content, the book is, however, a work of literature. The events recorded by Anne need not be examined for validity, nor can the point of view be assailed. It must also be kept in mind that this is a work in translation. Consequently, the various standards of literary criticism barely apply. Critical commentary must dwell on the work as a whole, passing judgment mainly on the effect of the writing rather than on style or content. The effect on most readers, naturally, is one primarily of sympathetic interest and identification because of the author's age and the circumstances under which the work was produced.

INITIAL ENDORSEMENT

The late Eleanor Roosevelt wrote the introduction to the first commercial edition which was published in 1952. She called the book "remarkable," accounting for her praise on the basis of the author's youth, candor, wit, and capacity for written expression. Mrs. Roosevelt also lauded the work because to her it represented and nobility of the human spirit in a time of human degradation and imminent destruction. The author herself was considered by Mrs. Roosevelt to be an outstanding example of the talented and sensitive adolescent with a concept of life from which people of all ages might enrich their own.

UNANIMOUS ACCLAIM

The reviews in such magazines as Time, Newsweek, and Commonweal were unanimously favorable. Once again, *The Diary of a Young Girl* received praise for the honesty and sensitivity with which it had been written. Anne's insight and maturity were also acclaimed. The emerging portrait of the author was once again the local point of the reviewers' attention. Lastly, the work was cited as a tribute to the over-all heroic spirit pervading the Diary.

STAGE AND SCREEN

When in 1955 the book was produced as a Broadway play under the title, *The Diary of Anne Frank*, it was again favorably reviewed. Adapted for the stage by Frances Goodrich and Albert Hackett, the script had undergone eight revisions before the playwrights were satisfied with their work. For their efforts and those others whose talents went into the acting and production, the play was rewarded in 1956 with the Antoinette Perry and Critics' Circle Awards as well as the Pulitzer Prize. Brooks Atkinson, then drama critic for *The New York Times*, wrote the introduction to the script which was published in book form. Commenting on the original Diary, Mr. Atkinson found the work an outstanding portrait of adolescence, enhanced by the surprisingly mature ideas of the author. He also noted the powerful philosophy of the will to survive exemplified by the work. Finally, Mr. Atkinson acclaimed it as a reminder, more accusing than formal documents, of Nazi atrocities.

In preparation for the CinemaScope motion picture version of *The Diary of Anne Frank* producer George Stevens traveled to Amsterdam in 1957 to interview Otto Frank. In reading the Diary, Mr. Stevens had been overcome by the irony of the little book's survival in spite of the Gestapo's avowed task to destroy all records of their deeds. From Mr. Frank the producer felt he could learn the answer to this curious quirk of fate. The Nazi officers had simply overlooked the cloth-covered book as a useless object. It is the survival of Anne's diary about which Mr. Stevens writes in his commentary-the beautiful irony which kept alive forever the belief of the young author that good will triumph over evil.

THE DIARY OF A YOUNG GIRL

ESSAY QUESTIONS AND ANSWERS

Question: Anne's relationship with her parents is a problem about which she is often disturbed. In what way does her attitude mature toward both her father and her mother?

Answer: When we first meet Anne she is going through what is known as the "Oedipal" stage according to many psychologists. This is manifested in the resentment she displays toward her mother and the preference she exhibits for her father. At this point, Anne is her mother's rival for Mr. Frank's love. There are many ways in which Anne excludes her mother from her affections. Among them are frequent instances of Anne's refusal to communicate with her mother, either by ignoring the woman's overtures of companionship, by arguing with whatever Mrs. Frank says about her behavior, or by excluding her mother from her confidence. Anne prefers to rely on her father for correction, companionship, and comfort. As she begins to feel ashamed of her attitude toward her mother, Anne examines the reasons for it. She comes to the conclusion that Mrs. Frank is a poor example of motherhood, especially since the woman considers her daughters more as friends, thereby failing to achieve the maternal authority and distinction which exist as the proper attributes of a mother in Anne's mind. Anne also feels that her mother is too frequently out of sorts and takes these moods out on her. Anne resolves to alienate herself permanently from her mother and to strive for total love and approval from her father. Discovering that the bond of love which exists between her parents is one which she cannot possibly damage, Anne withdraws from them both and feels deserted. She is determined to do her growing up by herself now. Ashamed of her own resentment, Anne attempts to feign a response to her parents even though she does not actually feel the warmth she displays. When she discovers that her parents' attitude is consistent and that hers is the one undergoing a change, she does some more serious thinking, and analyzes the situation again, giving particular consideration to her mother. The result is that Anne begins to perceive her mother as an individual with human shortcomings as well as some good qualities. She does regret, however, that her mother is not the ideal model that she herself would like to follow. By the same token, Anne also realizes that her father can never belong to her alone. In fact, now that she has Peter as a love object, she no longer wants her father in the old way. Caring for Peter has helped Anne realize how her mother must care for her father. This, in a sense, helps Anne to identify with womanliness, and causes her to be less resentful of her mother and other women in general. It is also possible now for Anne to understand the personality differences between herself and her mother, and in so doing she can accept the good and adjust to the bad qualities. Moreover, she no longer tries to force her mother into an ideal image which fails to live up to her former concept of perfection. With her parents in a more realistic perspective, Anne finds her relationships with both greatly improved.

Question: How do the members of this group in hiding seek positive means of fighting the pressures of confined living? Whose methods are most successful and why?

Answer: Since the occupants of the hiding place have been cut off from the customary forms of entertainment and participation in sports, the only remaining available outlets for all are listening to the radio, conversing, participating in domestic chores, and engaging in limited gymnastic exercises. The women are able to knit, sew, and clean; the young people have their learning activities; and the men may attend to the specialized functions of security and those few affairs of business for which they are still directly responsible. Nevertheless, the routine of sameness becomes unbearably boring and only extreme efforts of positive thinking make any activity seem really worthwhile. Too much thinking causes depression by drawing personalities into themselves with self-pity and despair over their plight the result. It is necessary for each person to find something to do of special interest so that the time will pass more meaningfully and so that the war outside the hideout and the conflicts within can be forgotten. For Anne, the hobbies she has acquired are very helpful. They include tracing the lineage of many European royal families, collecting pictures of film stars, learning different languages, practicing shorthand, helping with Elli's office work, and writing in her diary. This last project, while of great interest, and also valuable as an outlet for her emotions, often causes her to reflect even more unhappily on her problems. Margot pursues pretty much the same pattern of intellectual activity as Anne, finding an outlet in her mother's companionship, but also able to keep fairly much within herself. Peter has his cats on whom he showers affection, his studies and chores, and he manages to sleep off much of the frustrations of confined living. Mrs. Frank reads a great deal, sews, and finds comfort in her relationship with her husband and her older daughter. Mr. Frank has so much responsibility that he is often kept busier than his nerves can stand. His outlets are translating Dickens from English into German, working with his daughters on their projects, reading classical German drama aloud to those who wish to listen, and dabbling at composing poetry. Mr. Van Daan spends a good deal of his time keeping up with all sources of war information, studying maps, and working out theories of war strategy and politics. He also finds it calming to smoke cigarettes. Mrs. Van Daan's chief occupation is attending to domestic matters. Such activities as scrubbing, cooking, and cleaning help rid her of nervous energy. Mr. Dussel has his important project and although he is somewhat mysterious, most likely it concerns some aspect of dental science.

It is safe to say that those who are best able to utilize their mental resources have the advantage over those whose outlets are manual or primarily physical. The better able one is to devote oneself to a subject of study, the easier it is to forget unwanted thoughts. Mr. Frank seems to be the most adept at this form of mental escape, and Dussel is likely the next. Margot and Mrs. Frank are fairly well able to live with their own thoughts when not engaged in deliberate mental labor. Anne's imagination takes her out of herself, but as often as not, lands her in a nest of problems equally as disturbing as the ones she left behind. For both Anne and Peter, the best outlet is their relationship but that comes very late in the course of their life in hiding. Mr. and Mrs. Van Daan seem to have the least intellectual interests, and for that reason, often fall to bickering and complaining.

Question: What are the different sources of unpleasantness among the eight occupants of the hideout? How can they be explained and possibly condoned?

Answer: The sources of unpleasantness among the eight people in hiding can be divided into those which are common to all and others which are individual matters. The common sources of unpleasantness are quite numerous, readily understandable, and certainly forgivable. Quarters are cramped and the limitations of space make privacy and freedom of physical movement almost impossible. The sameness of routine is frustrating. Reports of the arrests, deportations, and deaths of Jews are extremely bad for the morale. Many of their friends and acquaintances number among the victims of Nazi persecution. The air raids are nerve-wracking and also prohibit sleep. Bombings nearby create terror because all realize there is no such thing as escape. Rations of food and other commodities fluctuate, often only from bad to worse. The fear of being discovered is always present and made even more real by frequent burglaries and suspicious people nearby. When illness strikes, a doctor may never be summoned and the home remedies relied upon take longer to effect cures. The general morale is subject to constant fluctuation between hope and despair depending on radio broadcasts of war news.

Individual problems are equally as difficult to solve as they are to live with. Personalities conflict: Mrs. Frank against Anne, Dussel versus Mr. Van Daan, Mrs. Van Daan versus Mrs. Frank, Mr. and Mrs. Van Daan against each other. Anne versus Margot, and the Van Daan family against the Franks. Certain habits of one person annoy the entire group: Mrs. Van Daan's coquetry and her hysteria, Anne's chattering and know-all attitude, Mr. Dussel's peevishness, and Mr. Van Daan's stubbornness. There is no day completely free of internal strife, nor is there any way to cope with difficulties of the outside world. Everyone longs to be free; the present is dismal and the future uncertain.

Question: In what ways do the other seven members of the group in hiding deal with Anne's precociousness, and what are possible reasons for their reactions?

Answer: Anne's superior intellect, her astute perception, and emotional sensitivity create problems for the others. Her father responds wisely and lovingly, accepting his daughter's precociousness more as a challenge than as a burdensome responsibility. To Mrs. Frank, Anne is unreachable, resentful, and often appears to be deliberately cruel. She is unable either to understand fully or cope more than partially with her daughters, sadly but wisely, she leaves Anne to her father for the guidance and affection the girl will accept only from him. Mrs. Frank's occasional harshness toward Anne grows out of a dual need both to protect her injured feelings and to defend herself in their subtle rivalry for Mr. Frank's love. Margot seems to ignore her younger sister, finding Anne' immaturities annoying and her advanced ideas not always of interest. Margot's cattiness toward Anne results from the natural rivalry between sisters and also is used as a weapon in defense of their mother against the younger girl's treatment. Dussel is flabbergasted by Anne as the product of progressive methods of upbringing. He is overwhelmed by the proportion of her mental and physical energy. He ignores her whenever possible and criticizes her when combat becomes inevitable. Peter is at first annoyed by Anne's childishness and ignores her after a few minor overtures of friendship. Later he secretly admires her humor, intelligence, and outward self-confidence, but remains aloof after her initial disinterest in him. When at last she seeks him out, he is as smitten as any young man by her feminine charm. He is reassured by her confidence and compassion, and respond even more fully than she to the longing for love that they share. Mr. and Mrs. Van Daan see Anne's precociousness as poor behavior resulting from a progressive upbringing. They seem unaware of her extraordinary qualifications for the most part, and interpret her words and actions negatively. Mrs. Van Daan is apt to feel intellectually inferior to Anne and Mr. Van Daan is aware of her low opinion of his stubbornness. Thus threatened, both react to her with criticism. Later on, after she has reconsidered her attitudes, she seeks the Van Daans on a level which make for certain areas of compatibility. It is then that she gains their moderate admiration for her superior qualities.

Question: How does Anne's independent spirit develop from outbursts of childish rebelliousness to a level of mature self-reliance?

Answer: From her pre-hiding days at the Jewish Lyceum, Anne's somewhat mischievous contempt for adult authority is directly dependent on her concept of ideal beings. If an adult falls short of her image of perfection, then that person's authority will be tested. The only grownup worthy of authority is her father who, Anne feels, is just such an ideal person. For those who do not measure up to Mr. Frank, Anne displays degrees of resentment according to the amount of authority being exercised and the way in which it is presented. Anne most often obeys, but she will question the purpose of the orders given. What she resents most, however, is criticism from those whose own imperfections are obvious to her. It is in this reaction to criticism from her mother, the Van Daans and Dussel that her rebellious outbursts are noticeable. For, rather than submit to rebukes and corrections, she will attempt to justify herself by mentioning not only all the reasons she is being unjustly criticized, but she will point out some flaws in her accuser. The result is usually calamitous. Feeling herself the victim of unfair criticism, Anne vows to win everyone's respect by a display of perfection and thus gain both independence and recognition as an equal in the eyes of her seniors. For a long period of time, Anne withdraws into herself to figure out how she can gain the desire advantage in these relationships without submitting completely to others' points of view or being so offensive in maintaining her own. The result she seeks is one that eventually establishes her as an independent being by giving her self-confidence and less resentment of authority.

After much pondering, followed by trial and error, Anne succeeds in achieving this independence, but only after she realizes that it is up to each individual to seek perfection in himself rather than force it in images upon others. When a person is responsible to oneself for achieving ideals and does not depend on others to live up to models of perfection, the shortcomings of others can be understood and forgiven. Recognizing this, Anne becomes more realistic in accepting others for what they are, while at the same time upholding a pattern of ideals to be followed by herself. Relying less upon others and more upon herself in this quest for idealism constitutes the source of Anne's independence. Her understanding of this gives her maturity through self-reliance, and wisdom comes from past experience. Hence, Anne achieves her independence by having reached a level of maturity on which she can stand secure in the approval of others that she has now earned.

Question: In what ways does the relationship between Anne and Peter result from a mixture of happy accident and obvious inevitability?

Answer: From deep in Anne's memory comes the strong emotion she felt for Peter Wessel, a friend from her former life on the outside. This emotion is renewed in a dream of such intensity that Anne awakens believing herself in love, with the image of Peter Wessel before her eyes, and the sensations of his touch still upon her cheek. Recognizing from her dream the deep longing to give and receive affection in a relationship with someone real in whom she can confide, Anne is determined to hold Peter Wessel as that ideal individual and to seek him in dreams whenever possible. That very day, however, she notices Peter Van Daan for the first time as a possible object of companionship. Until now the two have remained fairly aloof from one another. As she and Peter get to know one another better, they share their confidences and affections with each other in a relationship that is a mixture of friendship and romance. From time to time Anne writes in her diary that the images of Peter Wessel and Peter Van Daan have merged for her into one, but that the boy with whom she live is not as perfect as the one she recalls from her former life. The Peter of the past is still that mysterious hero of her dreams, but in reality it is Peter Van Daan with whom she shares her first real love experience even though she is disappointed in his faults. What has really occurred is that Anne, in her longing for a love object, has transferred her attention from the Peter Wessel of her imagination to the Peter Van Daan of reality. It is accidental only insofar as he is able to respond with mutual eagerness to Anne's need rather than to have found it in Margot, or to have remained locked within himself. The inevitability lies in Annes' own desire which was so strong and so intensive that it had to find an object. Having lost the youthful love ideal of her father, Anne was ready for a relationship in which she could fulfill someone else's need and find response in her own. Peter Van Daan was the most likely person in the group. Had he not been there, Anne would most likely have retained the fantasy of Peter Wessel as a love object. But the beauty of the relationship is in both Anne and Peter Van Daan. While she sought him initially and endeavored to make him care for her, his response was the fulfillment of both their needs to love and be loved.

Question: The five protectors typify those involved in the Dutch underground movement. What are the factors responsible for their attitude and activity regarding the eight occupants in particular and the "cause" in general?

Answer: More than any other European country occupied by the Nazis, the Netherlands is remarkable for the resistance shown by her citizens. The Dutch were particularly resentful of the anti-Semitic legislation enacted by Hitler and sought at first to counteract it by open opposition such as workers' strikes and violent propaganda in print. The Nazis in turn responded with harsh measures to punish the people and did so by shortening rations, altering the value of money, and restricting other privileges of Jews and Christians alike. Forced by the fear of doing further damage to innocent people, those anti-Nazi individuals known as "sympathizers" went "underground" and secretly worked for the destruction of the occupational forces while seeming on the surface to be passive to Hitler's troops.

So violent was the fervor of the underground that those involved were willing to take incredible risks for their own safety and well-being in order to destroy Nazi power. Much of this effort was extended to help Jews either to escape or to find safety in hiding. Either method required breaking the law and doing so under very close surveillance. Particularly ugly penalties were set up to punish crimes against the Fuehrer. Many services were performed for Jews by the sympathizers, such as procuring foreign documents, providing secret shelter, carrying or hiding possessions, and even transporting Jews to safety across borderlines.

Motivated by public spirit and private devotion, Miep, Henk, Elli, Kraler and Koophuis risked their lives daily as they undertook to protect the Franks, Van Daans, and Dussel for over two years. As the protectors had been associated with Mr. Frank's firm for several years, they were trusted with all business and personal matters. Their efforts were not unmarred by strain upon themselves and, in the end, Kraler and Koophius went to Nazi prison camps. Miep and Elli found Anne's diary and preserved it for Mr. Frank, the only survivor of the eight in hiding, who eventually had it published.

Question: In what way is Anne's diary indicative of her young age? Which aspects reveal a maturity beyond her years?

Answer: Anne's youth is apparent in the early pages of her diary in aspects of her style which indicate the awkwardness of a student wrestling with the rules of formal composition and at the same time attempting to free her mind of burdensome thoughts. The formality of her sentence structure negates the freedom of expression for which she strives in content. There is too, a noticeable jumping from topic to topic producing inconsistencies in tone, point of view, and over-all purpose. As the work progresses, however, the writing gains unity. Anne acquires experience in writing which helps her to lose the early formality that inhibited her wording and flow of ideas. Yet there are still evidences of extremes of mood and tone, which indicate her youthful lack of control. In contrast to these indications of immaturity, Anne's frequent comments on people, the war, and life in general reveal a wisdom and insight beyond her years.

By the second year, there are more noticeable changes in style and content. Anne's sentences have become more complex in structure. She has also acquired more self-assurance in handling her content. Another remarkable feature is the development of a more consistent philosophy of life and the obvious formation of firm set of values and ideals. The contradictions appear less as examples of clumsiness, and when there are inconsistencies, it is more likely to be the expression of Anne's many faceted personality. In style and in outlook. Anne's work shows growing maturity, often surpassing in depth of thought and honesty the work of many professional writers.

Question: The late Eleanor Roosevelt claimed that war's greatest evil was the degradation of the human spirit. Despite the experiences of Anne and the others recorded in her diary, why should this work be considered a triumph of the human spirit?

Answer: Between the ages of thirteen and fifteen, a Jewish girl named Anne Frank kept a diary which contained a record of her experiences and those of seven other Jews in hiding from the Nazis during World War II. Most of the events recorded took place in a hidden apartment on one of the canals in Amsterdam, Holland. Most of the action concerns the daily lives of these eight Jews in hiding and their five protectors-members of the Dutch underground. Other aspects of the diary are reports of war news and attempts to describe the process of the young author's development from childhood to young adulthood. For the most part, the book is of simple design, often repeating the same events and problems, but usually with fresh insight following much meditation. What complexities exist do so in the mind of the young author who eagerly seeks the meaning of man's life on earth through contemplation of his narrowest deeds and his mightiest thoughts.

Yet such a seemingly plain little book can represent a thing ten thousand times its appearance in depth of insight and breadth of scope. Despite the author's young age, her precocious intellect and unusual sensitivity have brought between the covers of this book a cameo in metaphor of man's struggle to know and understand, his will to survive, and his destiny to prevail.

The elements of good and evil are unevenly matched in a contest for survival. People are reduced from ordinarily happy and unassuming beings to desperate, hysterical creatures and ultimately to bones and ashes. These people are the 12,000,000 million enemies of one fanatic, and the author is a spokesman for the 6,000,000 who suffered and perished under his orders. The imbalance is not simply a numerical peculiarity, but an historical phenomenon unknown before and since. The book becomes, therefore, a monument not only to its author, her people, or a particular phase of recorded history but a monument attesting to the will of mankind to overcome evil and the destiny of the human spirit not only to survive, but to prevail.

BIBLIOGRAPHY

WORKS ABOUT THE JEWISH PEOPLE

History And Comment

Baron, Salo Whittmayer. *Social and Religious History of the Jews.* Rev. ed. 8 vol. New York; Columbia University Press, 1952. A comprehensive general history of the Jews from ancient through medieval times.

The Jews: Their History, Culture, and Religion, ed. Louis Finkelstein. 2 vols. New York: Harper & Brothers, 1949. An anthology of Jewish topics submitted by Jewish contributors from all fields.

Jews in the Modern World, ed. Jacob Freid. 2 vols. New York: Twayne Publications, Inc., 1962. An anthology of current written opinion on Jews by both Jewish and non-Jewish contributors.

Sachar, Abraham Leon. *A History of the Jews*, New York. Knopf, 1960. A comprehensive general history.

Anti-Semitism

Lea, Henry Charles. *The Inquisition of the Middle Ages: Its Origins and Operations.* New York: Citadel, 1961. A general study of the Spanish Inquisition.

Lea, Henry Charles. *The Moroscos of Spain: Their Conversion and Expulsion.* New York: Citadel, 1962. A study of the Spanish Inquisition in relation to the Jews.

Muhlen, Norbert. *The Supervisors.* New York: Thomas Y. Crowell, 1962. A report on Jews and Germany today. Reichmann, Eva G. *Hostages of Civilization.* Boston: Beacon Press, 1951. A study of the social causes of anti-Semitism in Germany.

Zionism

Buber, Martin: *Israel and the World.* "Essays in a Time of Crisis." New York: Schocken Books, 1948. Essays on the related topics of Israel, nationalism, and Zionism.

Lipsky, Louis. *A Gallery of Zionist Profiles.* New York: Farrar, Strauss, and Cudahy, 1956. Biographical sketches of the first and greatest leaders of Zionism.

WORKS ABOUT WORLD WAR II

History

Anderson, Eugene N. *Modern Europe in World Perspective 1914 to the Present.* New York: Rinehart & Co., Inc,., 1950. A comprehensive history of Europe from World War I through World War II.

Churchill, Winston. *The Grand Alliance.* Boston: Houghton-Mifflin, 1950. The war notes and memos of the late Prime Minister presented as an historical account.

Gunther, John. *Inside Europe Today*. New York: Harper & Brothers, 1940. A discussion of the politics, attitudes, and events recorded before America's entry into World War II.

Ryan, Cornelius. *The Longest Day*. New York: Simon & Schuster, 1959. An account of the D-Day landings.

Memoirs And Personal Accounts

LeVien, Jack and John Lord. *Winston Churchill: The Valiant Years*. New York: Random House. 1962. An account of Winston Churchill's role in World War II.

The Rommel Papers, ed. B. H. Liddell Hart, with the assistance of Manfred Rommel. New York: Harcourt, Brace & Co., 1953. The personal campaign diaries of Nazi commander Erwin Rommel (the "Desert Fox").

Meier, Maurice. *Refuge*. New York: W. W. Norton, Inc., 1962. The account of one man's ability to withstand oppression and to triumph over personal disaster.

Paller, Walter. Medical Block, *Buchenwald: The Personal testimony of Inmate 996, Block 36*. New York: Lyle Stuart, 1961. The point of view of a non-Jewish political prisoner.

Saint-Exupery, Antoine de. *Flight to Arras*. New York: Reynal and Hitchcock, 1943. The memoirs of a French flight officer.

Shirer, William. *Berlin Diary*. New York: Random House, 1948. A correspondent's account of wartime Berlin.

Masterpieces of War Reporting, ed. Louis Snyder. New York: Julian Messner, Inc., 1962. A collection of war correspondence, including entries by William Shirer, Ernie Pyle, John Steinbeck Ernest Hemingway, Andre Maurois, Rebecca West, Erskine Caldwell, and other well-known persons.

Unsdorfer, S. B. *The Yellow Star*. New York and London: Thomas Yoseloff, 1961. An account of the experiences sustained by a survivor of a Nazi concentration camp.

Hitler And The Nazis

Hilberg, Raul. *The Destruction of Jews*. Chicago: Quadrangle Books, 1961. A study in depth of Nazism begun during World War II.

Shirer, William. *The Rise and Fall of Adolf Hitler*. New York: Random House, 1961. An historical study in depth of Hitler's activities and their effects on the history of his time.

Shirer, William. *The Rise and Fall of the Third Reich*. A comprehensive study of the Germany of Hitler from its origins to the aftermath of World War II.

Tobias, Fritz. *The Reichstag Fire*. New York: G. Putnam's Sons, 1964. The story of the fire and subsequent trial that assured Hitler and the Nazis mastery over Germany.

Trevor-Roper, H. R. *The Last Days of Hitler*. New York: Macmillan, 1947. A documented study of the circumstances of Hitler's death and an examination of the mysteries surrounding it.

Waldman, Morris. *Seig Heil!* Dobbs Ferry, New York: Oceana Publications, Inc., 1962. A study in depth of Hitler and National Socialism.

War Crimes

Arendt, Hannah. *Eichmann in Jerusalem: A Report on the Banality of Evil.* New York: Viking Press, 1963. An exploration and analysis of the political philosophy underlying the trial of Adolf Eichmann in Israel.

Gallagher, Richard F. *Nuremberg: The Third Reich on Trial.* New York: Avon, 1962. The most complete study of the postwar trial of the German war criminals.

Heydecker, Joe J. and Johannes Leeb. *The Nuremburg Trials: A History of Nazi Germany as Revealed Through Testimony at Nuremburg*, ed. R. A. Downie. New York and Cleveland: World Publishing Co., 1962.

The Nurnberg Case, as presented by Robert H. Jackson, Chief Counsel for the United States. New York: Knopf, 1947. Testimony taken at Nurnberg accompanied by other documents Devil's Diary, ed. John L. Stapp. Yellow Springs, Ohio: Antioch Press, 1965. A record of Nazi conspiracy and agression.

RELATED WORKS

Anti-Semitism

Hersey, John. *The Wall*

Schwartz-Bart, Andre. *The Last of the Just*

Zionism

Uris, Jeon. *Exodus*

Drama Of The Jews And World War II

Hochhuth, Rolf. *The Deputy*

Miller, Arthur. *Incident at Vichy*